LOCOMOTION PAPERS

The Snape Branch

by
Peter Paye

THE OAKWOOD PRESS

© Oakwood Press & Peter Paye 2005

British Library Cataloguing in Publication Data
A Record for this book is available from the British Library
ISBN 978-0-85361-641-2

Typeset by Oakwood Graphics.
Repro by Ford Graphics, Ringwood, Hants.
Printed by Blissetts, Roslin Road, Acton, W3 8DH.

All rights reserved. No part of this book may be reproduced or transmitted in any form or by any means, electronic or mechanical, including photocopying, recording or by any information storage and retrieval system, without permission from the Publisher in writing.

Dedication

This book is dedicated to the late Doctor Ian C. Allen, who unofficially adopted the Snape branch as one of his own, and set about photographing the unusual railway byway at any available opportunity. We discussed the idiosyncrasies of the Suffolk branch lines over many lunches at his Thorpeness home and it is thanks to his generosity that most of illustrations in this volume were freely donated.

Snape River underbridge No. 1109 was used as a headshunt during shunting operations at Snape. Here 'J15' class No. 65478 backs her train of wagons into the yard. The tender is fitted with a back plate and a tarpaulin is stretched between the engine cab and tender to provide some protection for the footplate crew when running tender first. Note the winding course of the River Alde at this point as the photograph is taken from the riverbank. *The late Dr I.C. Allen*

Front cover: 'J15' class 0-6-0 No. 65389 on bridge No. 1109 on 3rd May, 1958. *R.C. Riley*
Rear cover: One of the problems encountered by the District Civil Engineer was the annual growth of weeds through the ballast and even a minor line like the Snape branch received the attentions of the weed killing train. 'J15' class 0-6-0 No. 65447 approaches Snape Junction with the train of six tanks containing the weedkiller, two associated ex-Southern Railway utility vans and brake van. Note the spray emanating from a rear SR vehicle on to the track. *The late Dr I.C. Allen*

Published by The Oakwood Press, 54-58 Mill Square, Catrine, KA5 6RD
01290 551122   www.stenlake.co.uk

Contents

	Introduction	5
Chapter One	History of the Line	7
Chapter Two	The Route Described	43
Chapter Three	Permanent Way, Signalling and Staff	59
Chapter Four	Timetables and Traffic	67
Chapter Five	Locomotives and Rolling Stock	85
Appendix One	Level Crossings	117
Appendix Two	Bridges	118
	Acknowledgements	119
	Bibliography	120

The Railway Enthusiasts' Club 'Suffolk Venturer' railtour train of 30th September, 1956 formed of five ex-LNER Gresley corridor coaches was hauled down the Snape branch by 'E4' class 2-4-0 tender locomotive No. 62797. After visiting the goods station, the locomotive propelled the stock back to the main line but was stopped on the approach to Snape Junction branch home signal to await the passing of the milk train from Halesworth. Having stopped on the 1 in 66/249 rising gradient, the engine was unable to restart the train and 'J15' class No. 65447 was sent to rescue the stranded special, causing some considerable delay to the itinerary. Here No. 62797 complete with express train headcode struggles with the train. The railway authorities, organisers and passengers must have thought the journey was jinxed for the locomotive had run short of steam with the train earlier in the tour on the relatively level gradient near Capel on the Hadleigh branch. *The late Dr I.C. Allen*

Title page: The rickety timbers of underbridge No. 1109 shudder under the 67 tons 15 cwt weight of 'J15' No. 65467 and her tender as she shunts wagons into Snape yard. Note the footpath crossing No. 6 where the towpath crossed the railway at 89 miles 29 chains.
The late Dr I.C. Allen

The ornate archway, complete with clock and bell tower, built by Newson Garrett in 1859. When the railway served the maltings a line passed through the arch. View taken in 1998. *Author*

Introduction

The internationally famous Aldeburgh Festival is firmly established in the world of arts and performances by famous artists, centred on the concert hall at Snape in June of each year, attract thousands to this Suffolk riverside retreat. The festival was founded in 1948 by the joint efforts of Benjamin Britten, Peter Pears and Eric Crozier. The initial performances were held in Aldeburgh Parish Church, the Baptists' Chapel and the Jubilee Hall, but as the festival's reputation grew so the arena of activities spread to the splendid churches at Framlingham, Blythburgh and Orford. As the years progressed and the repertoire further expanded, it was felt the venues were too fragmented and a central location was required.

By the early 1960s the need for a large permanent concert hall was paramount and plans were being considered to construct such a building in Aldeburgh, when the Snape Maltings complex came up for sale. A new company was formed to use the premises for corn storage but the scheme did not include the large building, known as the New House, behind the main block and, after investigation in 1965, the Festival authorities shelved the Aldeburgh plans in favour of this large malthouse. The following year a 50 year lease was signed. From there on with the aid of covenants, appeals and charitable trusts, enough money was raised to convert the building to a concert and opera hall. The walls of the malting building were extraordinarily thick, being constructed in the Old Flemish Bond, and Arup Associates designed the conversion. Aldeburgh brickworks supplied any new red bricks required, whilst the work was contracted to William C. Reade Limited, also of Aldeburgh. The task was completed in time for the first Aldeburgh Festival to be held at Snape in June 1967, only to be cruelly truncated when on the night of 7th June, 1969 the malthouse roof burnt down. The malthouse was quickly rebuilt in time to open at the start of the next season, since when the Festival has gone from strength to strength. Now concerts are held all year round, whilst other buildings have been converted into quality retail outlets.

With such a success story it is easy to overlook the fact that the Festival would not have been sited at Snape if a certain entrepreneur, Newson Garrett, had not taken over the area of huts at the navigable head of the River Alde in the 1840s and developed the site into the vast malting complex, which continued as an active industry for almost 120 years. Although Garrett initially relied on water and the primitive road transport of the day, much of his imports and exports were conveyed by rail along a short branch line, which from 1859 connected with the East Suffolk Railway (ESR). Garrett, with great foresight had negotiated with the company for the branch and for just over a century the Eastern Counties Railway (ECR) and later Great Eastern Railway (GER), London & North Eastern Railway (LNER) and finally British Railways, Eastern Region (BR ER) operated a goods train each weekday to serve the maltings and surrounding area. The railway thus had a great part to play in the evolution of Snape and its Maltings, ensuring the complex can be enjoyed by present and future generations. This volume gives the history of the short branch line from inception to closure in 1960, details have been checked with available documents, but apologies are offered for any errors, which may have occurred.

Peter Paye
Bishop's Stortford
2005

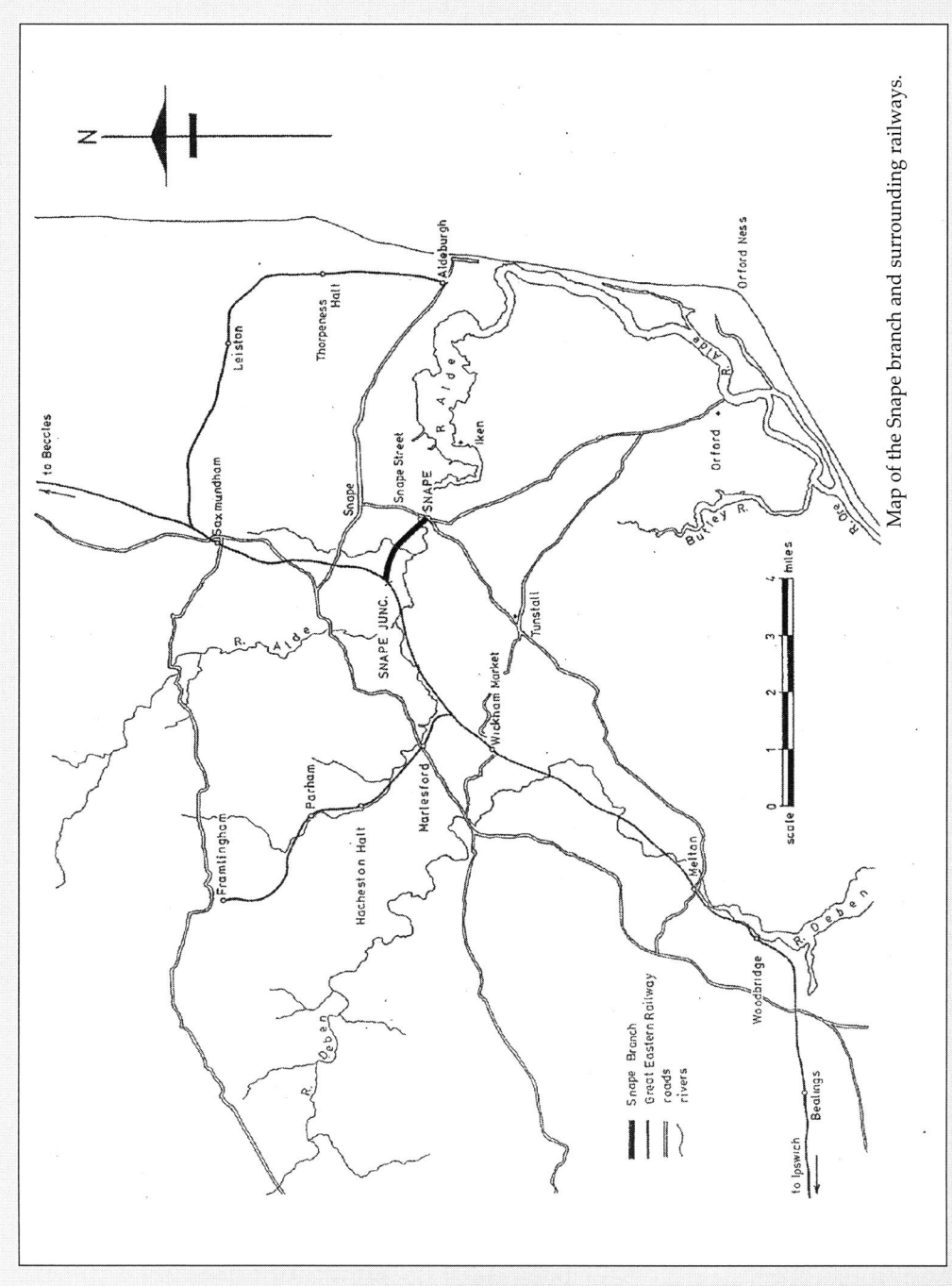

Map of the Snape branch and surrounding railways.

Chapter One

History of the Line

The River Alde rising near Brundish in the undulating hills of mid-Suffolk is an insignificant stream until it reaches Snape Bridge, five miles as the crow flies from the North Sea. Thereafter it takes a 20 mile meandering and tortuous course to reach the sea at Orford Haven. In its windings the river passes the old ports of Iken, Aldborough or Aldeburgh and the lengthy shingle bar where the Alde changes its name to the River Ore for its last few miles to salt water. In 1155 Benedictine monks established a priory on land just above the tidal head of the river, using boats to bring materials for the construction of the buildings. The establishment suffered under the dissolution of the monasteries and was demolished in 1562. At the same time King Henry VIII gave the adjacent Snape Manor to Cardinal Wolsey, who planned to use the rent from the property to help finance his great educational schemes. However, after he failed to get the papal blessing for the King's divorce Wolsey fell into disgrace and the manor returned to the crown. The quiet village of Snape, with its late 13th century church of St John the Baptist, lies a mile north of the winding tidal inlet but for centuries Snape Quay, alongside Snape Bridge spanning the Alde, has been the centre of activity as small boats plied their trade for the community. The anchorage, actually located in the parish of Tunstall, was ideal as a trading post being the highest point of navigation on the River Alde, dictated by the lowest bridging point on the river and on the seaward side of the bridge. The area was at one time famous for its horse trading, for Dunningworth Horse Fair was held annually in front of Dunningworth Hall on 11th August, the sale of the Suffolk Punch cart horses taking its name from the lost Domesday village of Dunningworth. Between 1727 and 1842 an annual horse race, over a distance of seven miles, was held at the Snape race course.

A few miles to the north of Snape, at Leiston an enterprising blacksmith Richard Garrett had in the early 18th century established an iron works, initially making blades and agricultural equipment for local farmers. Over the years the family business flourished and the undertaking was a thriving concern. The management of the engineering works was taken over by his son Richard but unfortunately there was no position for a younger son, Newson, who went to London to seek his fortune. Whilst in the capital he was at one time manager of a pawnbroker's shop in Whitechapel and later met, and subsequently married, Louisa Dunnell, whose family lived at Dunwich, near Southwold. On 9th June, 1836 Louisa gave birth to her second child Elizabeth, who later as Elizabeth Garrett Anderson was a powerful advocate for women's emancipation and suffrage, one of the first women to qualify as a doctor in Britain and the first woman mayor (of Aldeburgh).

At the beginning of the 19th century the partnership of Osborne and Fennell ran a corn and coal business at Snape Bridge, operating from the small quay with its attendant cottage and a few wooden sheds. The business served a considerable catchment area and Sir Charles Blois of Yoxford was a regular

Newson Garrett in his robes of office as Mayor of Aldeburgh. Garrett developed the area around Snape Bridge and from 1854 built up the maltings. He also negotiated with the East Suffolk Railway for the provision of the branch line to serve the industrial complex.

Suffolk Record Office

customer. In 1840 Fennell fell ill and it was decided to sell the business. The following year, on his elder brother Richard's advice, the 29-year-old Newson Garrett came home and bought out the undertaking using the small endowment inherited from his father who had died in 1837, also adding some money from the Dunnell family. The Sandlings, a surrounding area of light soil, was ideal for the cultivation of barley and Garrett decided to further his fortunes by establishing Snape as a trading outlet for growers of the district. By 1844 Garrett was benefiting from the increasing beer consumption in the capital and was buying and dispatching regular consignments of barley by sea to the London breweries. Such was the growth in trade, Newson decided that not only could he profitably export barley for malting at other locations, he could establish that lucrative business at Snape.

From 1846 local bricklayers, carpenters and other artisans were offered work, constructing malt houses and in 1851 Garrett enhanced his interest by acquiring shares in the Bow Brewery. In the same year he authorized the building, at Snape, of the first known 'Thames' type sailing barge of 51 tons displacement and named her *Argo*. In 1854 further buildings were constructed at Snape, the bricks used being manufactured in local brickfields, in which Newson also had a financial interest, the mellow red facing bricks being offset by yellow quoins. The locally grown barley was then turned into malt during the winter months and was shipped by sailing barges to the many London breweries located alongside the River Thames. The site rapidly expanded, not only with malt houses, for with the increased port facilities a carpenter's shop and smithy were also provided. The quay at that time could accept vessels of between 60 and 90 tons laden weight. From the outset Garrett operated a small fleet of 12 barges to transport the commodity to London and, as trade expanded, improved dock and repair facilities were constructed adjacent to the maltings. By 1855 Newson Garrett was established as a maltster, lime, coal and corn merchant, brick and whiting manufacturer and shipbuilder. Later he was registered as a maltster, corn and seed merchant, Lloyds agent and Receiver of Droits for the Admiralty. Despite reliance on river and sea transport, with the coming of the railways in East Anglia the entrepreneur realised he could ill afford to be divorced from the system, if his business was to survive.

The advent of the railways into East Anglia began in earnest with the incorporation of the Eastern Counties Railway on 4th July, 1836. With share capital of £1,600,000, the company had powers to build a 126 mile line from Shoreditch in East London to Norwich and Yarmouth via Colchester, Ipswich and Eye. By September £58,100 of shares had been sold but there was great concern that only a twelfth of the capital raised was of local origin. Construction commenced in late March 1837 at the London end only, as incomplete negotiations with landowners prevented a start being made concurrently at Norwich and Ipswich. The troubles continued when landowners along the proposed route demanded higher compensation, and by October 1838, with 40 per cent of the capital called, only nine miles of railway was under construction. With creditors pressing, urgent action was necessary to prevent total ruin and by April 1839 Lancashire proprietors, who had taken a majority stake in the undertaking, forced a decision to terminate the line at Colchester.

The first public trains ran from the temporary terminus at Mile End to Romford on 20th June, 1839, with extensions each end to Shoreditch and Brentwood opening for traffic on 1st July, 1840. Robert Stephenson was engaged by the ECR Directors to give engineering advice but he could only confirm that another £520,000 was required to complete the railway to Colchester. Mutinous shareholders were almost bludgeoned into meeting the calls for outstanding share capital and application was made to Parliament for a further £350,000 share capital in 1840. With these assets and the added borrowing powers authorized by the 1840 Act, construction of the final section went ahead. Eventually the line was opened to Colchester for goods traffic on 7th March, 1843, and for passenger trains on 29th March. The 51 mile line had taken seven years to construct at a cost of nearly £2½ million, the works alone amounting to £1,631,300 had exceeded the original estimate for the whole project from London to Yarmouth.

The ECR Directors decision to terminate the project at Colchester was of particular concern to the merchants of Ipswich and Norwich, who were fearful of isolation from the railway network. Some ECR shareholders from Norfolk and Suffolk alarmed by the slow progress and decision of April 1839, obtained a rule nisi in the Bail Court to force the fulfilment of the company's contract with the public, but this was overruled in 1840 when Parliament refused to extend the ECR powers beyond July of that year. Local factions then decided to take matters into their own hands by planning a railway linking Norwich with Yarmouth and this received the Royal Assent in 1842 to be followed in the next year by a projected line from Norwich to Brandon. By now Ipswich traders and businessmen were fearful of loss of trade. The situation was aggravated by the ECR plan to join up with the Norwich to Brandon line at Thetford, with the main line by-passing Ipswich altogether and leaving the town at the end of a branch line from Hadleigh.

Objections were made but ignored and so the traders and merchants of Ipswich produced their own scheme for a line linking the town with the ECR at Colchester. Plans were drawn up by Peter Schuyler Bruff, who had already worked on the surveys for the initial ECR route from London. The leading advocate of the Ipswich scheme was John Chevallier Cobbold, a member of the wealthy Ipswich banking and brewing family, who was a member of the original ECR Board of Directors. As well as connecting Ipswich with Colchester, the promoters of the scheme also intended to continue with a line running north to Norwich, and the new company entitled the Eastern Union Railway (EUR) was incorporated on 19th July, 1844.

In the meantime the ECR route to Thetford was abandoned but a group of businessmen in Bury St Edmunds were concerned their town would be isolated from the railway network. In February 1844 a deputation of interested parties met with the ECR Directors, to salvage the plans, but were advised the company was unwilling to extend its line beyond Colchester. The townsfolk subsequently promoted their own line, the East and West Suffolk Railway and were advised the EUR would not oppose the railway provided the route went from Bury St Edmunds to Ipswich via Hadleigh and not interfere with the direct line from Ipswich to Colchester.

The development of railways in Norfolk and Suffolk was the subject of a special study by the Railway Department of the Board of Trade and in a final report of 4th March, 1845 full support was given to the EUR scheme to Ipswich and for the extension to Norwich. The tract of land north-east of Ipswich towards Bury St Edmunds finally received the attention of railway developers with the passing, on 21st July, 1845, of the Act authorizing the construction of the Ipswich and Bury St Edmunds Railway. With an initial capital of £400,000 the new concern appeared nominally independent but was, however, an extension of the EUR, with no less that six EUR Directors appointed to a Board totalling 15 members. The Colchester to Ipswich section of the EUR was opened for goods traffic on 1st June and passenger traffic on 15th June, 1846, whilst the extension to Bury St Edmunds was opened to goods on 7th December and passenger traffic on 24th December, 1846.

Meanwhile in the autumn of 1845 a proposed railway to Hadleigh backed by the EUR had stemmed the competitive desire of the ECR to build a duplicate line from Colchester into East Anglia. Much to the annoyance of the Ipswich company, however, the ECR had not forsaken its goals of Norwich and Yarmouth but taken steps to reach Norfolk via an alternative route. On the same day as the ECR was incorporated in 1836, a rival company the Northern and Eastern Railway (N&E), received the Royal Assent to build a line over the 53 miles from Islington to Cambridge financed by a share capital of £1,200,000. As with the ECR, the N&E soon encountered financial difficulties and it was 1839 before construction commenced and even then only with the sanction of the ECR. To conserve finances the N&E route was diverted from Tottenham via Stratford, where running powers were permitted into the ECR Shoreditch terminus. Like the ECR the new line was built to a gauge of 5 feet and, despite the abandonment of the route north of Bishop's Stortford by Act of Parliament in 1840, had reached the Hertfordshire market town on 16th May, 1842, at a cost of over £25,000 per mile. In 1843 the N&E secured an extension Act for the line to Newport, some 10 miles nearer Cambridge, but on 23rd December of the same year the ECR agreed terms for a 999 years lease for the company from 1st January, 1844. Once the lease was in force, the ECR obtained powers for a line linking Newport to the Norwich & Brandon Railway at Brandon on 4th July, 1844. The N&E line, like the ECR, was converted to the standard gauge of 4 feet 8½ inches in the late summer of the same year and after a formal opening the previous day, the whole line from Bishop's Stortford to a temporary terminus at Norwich (Trowse) commenced public service on 30th July, 1845. The southern railway approach to Norwich was surveyed by Joseph Locke and built by the EUR. It ran from a junction with the Bury St Edmunds line at Haughley, north-west of Stowmarket and ran direct to the Norfolk capital via Diss. The line was opened in stages, initially for goods traffic to Finningham from 7th June, 1848, then to Burston for goods on 11th June and passengers from 2nd July, 1849, with completion by 7th November of the same year. Thus while the main routes from London to Norwich via Cambridge and Ipswich were established, the coastal area of Suffolk was devoid of railways.

The genesis of the branch railway to Snape Maltings began in 1851 when a local venture, known as the Halesworth, Beccles & Haddiscoe Railway

ANNO DECIMO SEPTIMO & DECIMO OCTAVO

VICTORIÆ REGINÆ.

✦✦✦

Cap. cxix.

An Act for making a Railway in Deviation and Extension of the *Halesworth, Beccles, and Haddiscoe* Railway from *Westhall Low Common* to *Woodbridge*, and certain Branches therefrom, and for changing the Name of the Company to the *East Suffolk* Railway Company.

[3d *July* 1854.]

WHEREAS an Act was passed in the Session of Parliament held in the Fourteenth and Fifteenth Years of the Reign of Her present Majesty, called "The *Halesworth, Beccles, and Haddiscoe* Railway Act, 1851," whereby the *Halesworth, Beccles, and Haddiscoe* Railway Company were incorporated and authorized to make a Railway from the *Lowestoft* Railway at *Haddiscoe* in the County of *Norfolk*, by *Beccles*, to *Halesworth*, with a short Branch to the *Lowestoft* Railway in the Parish of *Haddiscoe*, and such Railway is now in course of Construction between the Terminus at *Haddiscoe* and a Place called *Westhall Low Common* in the Parish of *Westhall* in the County of *Suffolk*: And whereas the making of a Railway in Extension of the said Railway from *Westhall Low Common* aforesaid to near the Town of *Woodbridge* in the County of *Suffolk*, with Branch Railways or Tramways therefrom to *Leiston*, *Snape Bridge*, and *Framlingham*, would be of great public and local Advantage; and the said *Halesworth, Beccles,*

14 & 15 Vict. c. xxvi.

[*Local.*] 21 G and

East Suffolk Railway Act of 3rd July, 1854, which amongst other things sanctioned the building of the Snape branch.

(HB&HR), started filling in this gap by obtaining powers to connect the river ports of Halesworth and Beccles with the Reedham to Lowestoft line of the Norfolk Railway. This line had been sanctioned as the second stage of the Lowestoft Railway and Harbour scheme in 1845 and was opened to goods on 3rd May, 1847 and for passengers on 1st July of the same year. In 1852 the HB&HR was empowered to enter into a working agreement with the Norfolk company and was subsequently opened to goods on 20th November and passenger traffic on 4th December, 1854. The Eastern Counties Railway, which had leased the Norfolk Railway in 1848, operated the line from the outset and by June 1855 the company was able to show a modest profit of £528. In the meantime, however, the HB&HR Directors, encouraged by the backing they had received, proposed a southward extension to Woodbridge to join up with the EUR. This EUR connection from Ipswich, originally proposed in 1847, was never built, and so these plans were also dusted down and resurrected in the hope the combined railways would provide a through route to the Suffolk capital and chief port of the county. At the same time it was proposed to rename the HB&HR undertaking, the East Suffolk Railway. Sir Samuel Morton Peto, who had ambitious schemes afoot to elevate the status of Lowestoft, immediately recognised the new line would provide a more direct access to London than the existing routes via Norwich. He quickly became the principal subscriber and subsequently offered to lease the whole line for 14 years on a cost not exceeding £10,000 per mile, with 3½ per cent paid during construction.

The proposals for both the EUR and ESR schemes, together with plans and books of reference were deposited with the Parliamentary Private Bill office on 30th November, 1853, with copies sent to parish councils affected by the planned railways. Included in the ESR proposal were branch railways to serve Richard Garrett's engineering works at Leiston and Newson Garrett's maltings at Snape Bridge. These were included to secure the support of the Garretts, by now influential in the district, as well as tapping useful sources of freight traffic for the railway. The brothers had guaranteed they would provide regular goods traffic to the company in return for direct access to the main line. This was especially relevant to Newson Garrett, whose perishable products would benefit from faster transit than that offered by sailing barges, as well as offering scope to expand his markets for barley and malt.

The ECR Directors, however, objected vehemently to the schemes and sent their General Manager to public meetings to argue against the proposals. The new line would in effect drain traffic from the Ipswich to Norwich line via Haughley, which the ECR, after taking all steps to destroy when in EUR hands, now controlled. Realising they were losing the battle the ECR officers astutely altered their strategy and agreed to work the new East Suffolk line, but without the financial guarantees applicable to the original Halesworth to Haddiscoe section, thus ensuring a controlling power.

The vesting of all assets of the Halesworth, Beccles & Haddiscoe Railway to the newly titled East Suffolk Railway was duly authorized by the East Suffolk Railway Act (17 and 18 Vict. cap. cxix), which received the Royal Assent on 3rd July, 1854. The statute also sanctioned the extension of the main line authorized in 1851 on to Woodbridge and the construction of three branch railways or tramways; the first from a junction at Saxmundham to Leiston with an extension to the Manufactory of Richard Garrett in Leiston and the second from a junction on the main line in the Parish of Campsey Ash to Framlingham. The third branch railway or tramway commenced by a junction with the main line in the Parish of Farnham, in the County of Suffolk and terminated in the Hamlet of Dunningworth in the Parish of Tunstall in the same county near Snape Bridge. As with the other branches, three years were permitted for the compulsory purchase of land for the Snape branch and five years for the completion of works. Clause xliii authorised the provision of level crossings over public highway No. 12 in the parish of Tunstall and hamlet of Dunningworth in Tunstall and public highway No. 33 in the parish of Snape. The company was required to provide a station or lodging for a crossing keeper adjacent to these crossings.

The share capital of the new company for the new schemes was £450,000, formed of £150,000 shares of the former Haddiscoe company and £300,000 new shares. The company was authorised to borrow £50,000, once half of the original capital had been paid up. The first Directors of the new company were Edward Leathes, Andrew Johnston, Richard Till, James Peto, Holland Thomas Birkett and George Teed. George Berkley of 24 Great George Street, Westminster, London was appointed Engineer to the company,

On 22nd February, 1855 Sir Samuel Morton Peto estimated the cost of the Halesworth to Woodbridge line at £194,686 2s. 6d. or £8,812 per mile with principal stations at Halesworth and Saxmundham and cheaply built minor stations at Melton, Campsea Ashe, Snape and Bramfield. The 1 mile 32 chains branch to Snape Bridge was costed at £10,601 12s. 7d., an exorbitant £6,812 per mile, compared with £8,064 for the Framlingham branch and £6,109 for the short line to Leiston. At a subsequent meeting of the Special Joint Committee of the Eastern Counties Railway, the Norfolk Railway and the Eastern Union Railway held on 11th May, 1855 G.P. Bidder, the ESR Consulting Engineer, reported the final costs of the proposed lines were not yet available. This, despite having submitted a written report from his office at 24 Great George Street, Westminster on 5th May, 1855, with the estimated cost of the line and the three branches concurring with the figures given by Peto in February. The meeting considered the facts of the report. As well as others, it was proposed Snape should have a station equal to the accommodation of the expected traffic, and that after deduction of working expenses it would contribute towards the payment of five per cent on the cost of the construction of the overall railway. It was announced that 12 acres of land would be required to build the Snape branch.

The district served by the ESR was approximately 450 square miles bordered on the east by the coast, on average six miles distant, whilst 15 miles to the west was the EUR linking Ipswich and Norwich. At the northern extremity were the towns of Lowestoft and Bungay and to the south the River Deben. The acreage of the land was 493,471, with a population as recorded in the 1851 census of 104,760. Chief watering places were at Aldeby and Southwold whilst the three ports of Aldborough, Snape and Woodbridge served the area. Bidder considered it was an 'absolute condition' that only the main line should be constructed as priority with the branches as an optional extra. The three members of the Joint Committee, R. Moseley, Charles Capper and A.G. Church begged to differ, and considered the main lines would best be served by the feeder lines and all constructed together. In conclusion it was noted that coastal shipping using Aldborough and Snape Bridge during 1854 totalled 178 vessels arriving, with a gross load of 13,000 tons and 103 vessels embarking, with 6,000 tons of traffic.

The ECR had initially considered taking over the ESR but at the ECR shareholders' meeting on 13th July, 1855, Mr Bruce, a Director, opposed the idea saying the ECR shareholders would lose money if the takeover was made. He was severely critical of the report made by the ECR officers on the prospects for the East Suffolk line saying they had omitted Snape and Aldeburgh when calculating the effects of local ports on the railway. They had also optimistically forecast that all the Snape Maltings traffic would be transferred from barges to rail traffic, but Bruce warned against this assumption and was later proved correct. He also claimed the estimate of 104,760 persons in the catchment area of the railway was 15 per cent too high. David Waddington, the ECR Chairman, counteracted that if they did not make the line other parties would. Mr Lewin, a shipper of flour from Woodbridge, stated he had traded for the past 40 years and fully advocated the building of the railway. After further discussion Bruce won the day and the shareholders were sent further information on the line so they could reach a decision. The shareholders duly endorsed the doubts of Bruce and rejected takeover, leaving the ESR to finance the building of the line. The Norfolk Railway Directors also met on the same day and reported the cost of constructing the ESR would reach £10,000 per mile.

The ESR Company issued its Prospectus on 1st September, 1855 and estimated revenue of £48,014, by comparing the amount of trade in East Suffolk with that in other areas already served by railways. It stressed passenger revenue would be £22,261 and goods receipts £25,753, whilst the operating costs were expected to be 46 per cent of receipts with the debt interest on the construction of the line a mere five per cent. The initial working profit of 54 per cent was, however, to be largely swallowed up paying off miscellaneous debts. Local traffic alone was expected to pay a five per cent dividend. The ESR Prospectus still expressed the promoters' desire for the ECR to take over the concern but because of the ECR shareholders' decision, the ESR Directors begged the ECR to help and the request was conveyed via an intermediary, J.C. Cobbold, the EUR Chairman, whose company was already controlled by the ECR. The ECR Directors, however, refused to contribute towards the construction of the ESR line and the local Directors were forced to raise a sum of £600,000, a figure £150,000 in excess of the share capital authorized in the 1854 Act.

The ECR authorities initially had no qualms with Sir Samuel Morton Peto's subscription to the ESR Woodbridge extension, but when in 1856 two newly-authorized companies backed by Peto, the Yarmouth & Haddiscoe Railway (Y&H) and the Lowestoft & Beccles Railway (L&B) accepted his proposals to lease them for 21 years at six per cent their suspicions were aroused. At the same time Peto was showing interest in making a line from Pitsea, on the

London, Tilbury & Southend Railway, which he already leased, to Colchester, from where running powers would be sought over the EUR to Woodbridge. By such means it was possible for a competitive service to run from London to Yarmouth and Lowestoft in direct opposition to the ECR. Fortunately the Pitsea to Colchester line was never built but the process of amalgamating the Y&H and L&B with the ESR in 1856 was the start of grandiose plans. Later Peto revised his terms with the ESR so that the whole line would be leased for 21 years, with six per cent paid from 1st July, 1857, whether open to traffic or not, on the undertaking that double track was provided from Yarmouth to Woodbridge but leaving the Lowestoft to Beccles and the Leiston, Snape and Framlingham branches as single lines. The contract for building the railway and branches was duly awarded to Peto, Brassey and Betts.

At the half-yearly meeting of shareholders held on the last day of February 1857 at the Angel Inn, Halesworth, Berkley, the company engineer reported the main line was laid out and construction well advanced. Negotiations had commenced for the acquisition of land for the Framlingham, Leiston and Snape branches. Newson Garrett reported to the gathering that he had walked over the route and expressed his completed satisfaction with the works. In early June, the *Ipswich Journal* reported, 'Between two million and three million bricks, intended for the various bridge and station works, had been landed at Woodbridge'. They had been purchased at Harwich and transported round the coast by barge, having originated from brickyards in the London area. At the beginning of July 1857 a 'highly finished' locomotive arrived at Halesworth from Birkenhead, to be used on ballasting work on the main line between Saxmundham and Woodbridge, and also the three branch lines.

By August 1857, all cuttings and embankments on the main line were completed and four-fifths of the bridges had been constructed. Nine miles of the formation had been ballasted and eight miles of track laid. On 7th October the *Suffolk Chronicle* reported a journey along the line, when its reporter was conveyed in a horse-drawn wagon from Woodbridge to Ufford Bridge. Here there was a break in the line, as the land required for the railway had only recently been purchased. The journalist then walked the three miles to Campsea Ash where he joined another train hauled by a steam locomotive, which took him on to Saxmundham. He then journeyed to Snape where he was entertained to dinner by Newson Garrett and his son. By this time the bridge spanning the River Alde had been erected on the adjacent Snape Bridge branch.

At the half-yearly meeting of the ESR shareholders held at the end of February 1858, George Berkley, the Engineer, reported the main line was nearly completed. Rails were laid along the whole length of the Snape branch and the line was awaiting ballasting. The other branches were not as advanced, for Berkley stated permanent way materials had been provided for the Leiston branch, whilst earthworks and bridges on the Framlingham branch were in a forward state. The Directors optimistically announced that the main line and branches to Snape Bridge and Leiston would open in July, with Framlingham following in September. The Chairman stated he had, with others, recently travelled the 15 miles from Halesworth to 'where the branch turned off for Snape Bridge' and expressed satisfaction at the standard of construction.

The ESR Directors' optimism for the July opening of the main line and branches continued throughout the spring but was rudely shattered when the ECR Directors visited the various construction sites on the East Suffolk Railway on 3rd and 4th June, 1858. Accompanied by Owen, the ECR company Secretary and Robertson, the superintendent of the line they found the works were far from complete, whilst the connecting EUR line from Ipswich was also behind schedule. On the first day travelled to Ipswich by the 4.30 pm express from Shoreditch, whence they journeyed by road to Woodbridge. The next morning the party travelled to see the partially-built station at Campsey Ash before continuing to Snape, where they had a brief meeting with Newson Garrett and visited the maltings established alongside the River Alde at the limit of its tidal flow at Snape Bridge.

In the early months of 1859 rumour and counter-rumour were rife on the opening date for the ESR main line and branches. On 5th February it was said the line would be opened completely at the beginning of March as station masters and other officials were appointed, but four days later 'Indignant Shareholder' complained to the *Ipswich Journal* that he understood the line was to be opened for goods traffic only. By 19th February the press prophesied 'much anxiety would be voiced' at the half-yearly meeting to be held at Halesworth on 25th February, as the railway would not open on 1st March, and June or July were the expected dates for opening to passenger traffic. 'Unless something satisfactory was announced' Sir Samuel Morton Peto would 'have to run the gauntlet of fierce determined opposition from shareholders'.

On Friday 25th February, 1859 as a prelude to the meeting, the company through Mr Lockey, the sub-agent of the contractors Peto, Brassey and Betts, arranged with the ECR to run a special train from Woodbridge to take shareholders and other interested parties to Halesworth. The special, formed of an engine and 12 first class coaches conveying amongst others Sir Samuel Morton Peto and Mr Wagstaff, the company solicitor, departed at 10.00 am, and stopped initially at Campsea Ash station before traversing the Framlingham branch. After returning to the main line, the train made a momentary halt at Snape Junction so that passengers could view the completed goods line before continuing on to Saxmundham and Halesworth. At the meeting, chaired by the Earl of Stradbroke and attended by Richard and Newson Garrett, the ESR company Secretary W. Day announced the main line and branches were completed and ready for inspection. Notice had been given to the Board of Trade, and by 2nd March, 1859 arrangements were made for two heavy locomotives to be available for the inspecting officer's visit the following Thursday. Sinclair, the ECR locomotive superintendent was also delegated to attend.

Captain H.W. Tyler conducted the official Board of Trade (BOT) inspection of the main line between Woodbridge and Yarmouth, together with the branches to Framlingham, Snape, Leiston and Lowestoft, on Thursday 7th March, 1859. The inspector noted the permanent way of the Snape branch was similar to that used on the main line for part of the section, whilst the remainder was similar to that used on the Framlingham branch. Tyler found the earthworks of the branch were standing well and noted the sharpest curve on the line, near Snape Junction, was of 16 chains radius. The bridges, constructed of timber and

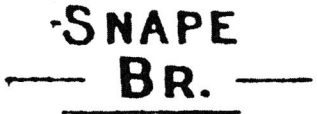

Gradient Profile of the Snape branch.

brickwork, were generally satisfactory but the small viaduct of 15 feet span required strengthening. The inspector was critical of the means of communication between the gateman of a level crossing who was 'appointed under "peculiar arrangements" to work the distant signals at Snape Junction', and the signalman at the junction 'who had charge of the main line signals and certain of the points'. He also required clocks to be supplied to all stations including Snape. Tyler required the company to furnish him with a certificate advising the method of the safe working of the single lines. Because of the incompleteness of the works the opening of the lines offered for inspection was refused. Within days Berkley, working closely with the contractors, arranged for the remedial works to be put in hand.

At a special meeting between the Directors of the ECR and ESR on 8th April, Sir Samuel Morton Peto was handed copies of the proposed timetables and passenger fares lists, and noted the goods cartage rates would be forwarded within a few days. It was agreed that ECR staff appointed to the new stations, including Snape, would take up their duties for the opening on 1st May, 1859. Indeed on Monday 18th April, all men appointed as station masters, clerks, porters and signalmen were taken to the various stations by Mr Dutton, traffic superintendent, and advised of their future role. Although the ECR had taken action to staff the ESR stations, matters at Woodbridge were far from complete, forcing the *Ipswich Journal* of 23rd April, 1859 to comment, 'It is now apparent the line will not open at the end of the month'.

Progress on the remedial works were so advanced that on 26th April, 1859 the ECR announced a special train would run the following day to deliver stores and furniture to all branch stations including Snape. Behind the scenes, however, many shareholders and local traders and businessmen were highly critical of the delay in opening the line, as nearly two months had passed since the BOT inspection. To silence the critics the company took the unusual step of publishing an extract of a letter dated 3rd May from Berkley, the company Engineer, in the *Ipswich Journal*:

> Captain Tyler has today seen that the slight alterations he required to be made to some of the signals have been completed. You will be aware that these were made nearly two months since but we waited until he was in the neighbourhood in inspecting the line from Ipswich to Woodbridge before they could conveniently be seen by Captain Tyler.

Captain H.W. Tyler had indeed re-inspected the East Suffolk main line and branches and in his report of 5th May, 1859 noted all the requirements made in his earlier report had been completed. He had received an undertaking signed by the Chairman and Secretary of the company that only One Engine in Steam would be allowed on the single line branches at any one time. Having received this assurance the inspector duly sanctioned the opening of all lines, including the Snape branch.

Some time elapsed, however, and it was 27th May before the ECR announced that the ESR main line and branches to Framlingham, Leiston and Snape would be opened for traffic on and from Wednesday 1st June, 1859. The Snape line from the outset was for goods traffic only but without the proposed passenger station at Snape Junction. The company must have had intentions of building the station for a made-up road was laid to the site, whilst details were included in *Bradshaw's Railway Guide* (*see page 66*) and local timetables for the East Suffolk line until 1863. The Woodbridge to Ipswich section built by the EUR opened on the same day, with all services operated by the ECR. To Newson Garrett, Snape Maltings was more than an industrial complex earning money, it was his personal status symbol. Thus in 1859, to coincide with the opening of the branch railway, he had had constructed a stylish arch with ornate frontage, through which wagons would be shunted into the premises. His business was by now registered at 61 Mark Lane, London EC but Newson Garrett continued to live close to his empire. He had built a low white house near Snape church, about a mile from the maltings, where he resided with his wife, and ultimately 10 children, between October and May, to be on hand for the winter malting. During the remaining months of the year the family returned to their house, initially Uplands and later Alde House, at Aldeburgh.

Wholly satisfied with the opening of their railway, the ESR Directors held a banquet at Lowestoft on Tuesday 14th June, 1859. Sir Samuel Morton Peto chaired the official proceedings following the meal and the usual complimentary speeches. Amongst those attending were the Earl of Stradbroke, Lord Paget MP, Horatio Love and J.C. Cobbold respective Chairmen of the ECR and EUR, together with the ECR Engineer Robert Sinclair and Peter Bruff, his counterpart on the EUR. Newson Garrett was also invited, in token of his backing for the railway and his intention to transfer much of his trade to rail. Despite the opening to traffic, considerable minor works had yet to be finished and on 22nd June, 1859, the ECR authorities agreed to convey all materials required for completion of the lines over their system free of charge. Richard Garrett & Sons provided a miscellany of items for the new railway from their Leiston works, including lamp posts, ironmongery, and general ironwork to the value of £4,300.

The Snape branch was initially worked by one of the three freight trains running between Ipswich and Yarmouth but from 2nd September, 1859 this was reduced to two trains in each direction. The resultant reduction meant it was no longer economic for one of these trains to work the branch, and it was suggested the Framlingham branch engine could work the services to and from Wickham Market station goods yard. Traffic would then be transferred to and from the through Ipswich to Yarmouth goods trains at Wickham Market. This arrangement was apparently unmanageable and inconvenient as Newson Garrett complained of delays to both incoming and outgoing traffic. At a meeting of the ECR and ESR Joint Committee on 24th September it was confirmed the Snape branch would be served by two goods trains daily.

The ESR Directors were disturbed by the anomalies in the charges for goods traffic, especially when conveyed to or from destinations on the ECR. The Earl of Stradbroke suggested at a meeting on 7th December, 1859 that all ESR traffic returns should be passed through the Railway Clearing House to negate any dubiety. Little progress was made, however, for at the half-yearly meeting held on Wednesday 5th March, 1860, Newson Garrett complained that the cost of the conveyance of coal was exorbitant and consequently traffic had not developed because of the high rates charged by the ECR. Because of the high charges he was still conveying coal to Snape by barge, as it was 'cheaper than conveyance by rail'!

On 18th July, 1860 a portion of ESR land was declared surplus to requirements at Snape and was offered to Newson Garrett on long-term lease. In the same month the inhabitants of Snape and surrounding area sent a memorandum to the ESR asking for a passenger train service across the branch. The matter was passed to the ECR and discussed at the meeting of the Joint Committee on 29th August, 1860. The appellants were later advised that after consideration it was 'not deemed expedient to increase the present service' of goods trains on the branch. In the same month Garrett expressed dissatisfaction with the service, which had again been reduced to one train a day, and requested additional trains to serve his maltings. The ECR traffic superintendent advised that extra services would cost more to run than receipts earned from existing traffic, and the request was curtly declined. Garrett was infuriated at the decision and took immediate steps to find alternative methods of transportation. He also encouraged other traders to follow his example. Because of the poor service, much of the incoming traffic continued to be brought by sea and delivered to the wharf at Snape for onward transit by horse and waggon. Newson Garrett had by no means finished with his complaining of the abysmal service provided by the ECR. Early in January 1862 he said that there had been no wagons at Snape available for loading on 24th December, 1861, as no trains had run to or from the station between 20th and 24th December. On the same day he found he had grain waiting in transit at other ESR stations, which was one week overdue for delivery to his maltings at Snape. The local railway managers refuted the allegations and the matter was passed to the ECR/ESR Joint Committee for discussion. Moseley, the traffic superintendent, stated the charges made were groundless. The matter had been brought before the Traffic Committee on 15th January and he had advised Garrett accordingly. The ECR authorities, initially unaware of the drain in trade and reduction of receipts brought about by the poor service and consequential transfer of trade to shipping, reacted in February 1862 by instructing the goods manager to counteract the competition by adjusting the rates and charges so that they were more beneficial to Garrett. At the same time the superintendent was instructed to improve the timekeeping and operation of the branch freight services in order to recover the traffic. The action was essential, for Garrett was sending and receiving commodities by sea using his own vessels sailing from Snape and Woodbridge to London, traffic which should have been conveyed by rail across the Snape branch. It even transpired that Garrett was paying no wharfage dues at any of the quays. A further dispute arose over the use of ECR company sacks, which Newson Garrett handed to farmers to fill with grain, supposedly for onward transit by rail to the maltings at Snape or to London. As a result of the problems encountered with rail transit Garrett was sending grain in ECR sacks by sea, a fact, which only became evident in early May 1862. The matter was brought before the ECR Traffic Committee at their meeting on 21st May, when it was resolved that ECR sacks could in future only be filled by farmers at stations and forwarded to their destination by rail. Garrett was duly informed of the ruling and asked to return surplus sacks to the railway

Down. Snape Branch.—(Single Line.)

Week Days.

Mile from Snape Jun	FROM	1 Gds. a.m.	2 Gds. p.m.	3	4	5	6	7	8	9	10	Sundays. 11	12	13	14
—	Snape Junction..........	10 40	4 30	...	...	...	...	...	...	...	...	...	...	...	...
1¾	Snape	10 45	4 35	...	...	...	...	...	...	...	...	...	...	...	...

The load of Goods Trains on this Branch is restricted to 15 Trucks.
No. 2 runs on Mondays, Wednesdays, and Fridays only.

Up.

Week Days.

Mile from Snape.	FROM	1 Gds. a.m.	2 Gds. p.m.	3	4	5	6	7	8	9	10	Sundays. 11	12	13	14
—	Snape	11 0	4 50	...	...	...	...	...	...	...	...	...	...	...	...
1¾	Snape Junction..........	11 5	4 55	...	...	...	...	...	...	...	...	...	...	...	...

No. 2 runs on Mondays, Wednesdays, and Fridays only.

GER Working Timetable 1862.

company. The smooth operation of the branch was not helped by the lack of the telegraph, which had been withdrawn from the line in the spring after Robertson reported it was underutilised.

Having leased or taken over the working of all the major railways in East Anglia, the ECR was the principal party to the scheme being prepared for the amalgamation of the Eastern Counties, Eastern Union, East Anglian, Newmarket and Norfolk Railways into a new undertaking known as the Great Eastern Railway. The Act sanctioning the amalgamation - the Great Eastern Railway Act 1862 (25 and 26 Vict. cap. ccxxiii) received the Royal Assent on 7th August, 1862, but took effect retrospectively from July of that year. By agreement the ESR was also amalgamated into the GER with effect from the date of the passing of the Act. The inhabitants of Snape and surrounding villages and hamlets could hardly wait for the new authority to take over, for within days a memorandum was sent to the Bishopsgate headquarters requesting the establishment of a passenger service on the branch. The application was considered on 20th August, 1862 but a decision was deferred.

As a result of the takeover, ESR proprietors were awarded £340,000 in GER 4 per cent debentures and £335,000 in 4½ per cent preference shares, as well as ordinary shares to the value deemed appropriate to future revenue expectations by Captain Galton of the Board of Trade. In return the GER was indemnified against the £86,488 contract debt and other liabilities of the company.

In April 1863 the GER General Manager submitted a notice of arbitration received from the company solicitor regarding Newson Garrett's claim of the agreement between himself and the East Suffolk Railway Company, which he wished to continue with the GER. With minor alterations to the wording, the revised document was duly agreed and signed.

Further representations for a passenger train service were regularly made and on 17th August, 1864 the GER Traffic Committee asked the superintendent to investigate the possibility of attaching mixed class carriages to the two daily goods trains 'for the accommodation of passengers desiring transit'. The officer duly investigated, and reported on 31st August that the timetable of the goods trains on the branch was not suitable for persons wishing to travel. He considered the only means of working the passenger traffic was by provision of an engine and passenger stock specially allocated to the line and the erection of a proper station and platform. The receipts from such a venture would barely cover the costs of working the branch, which was only 1½ miles in length. It was resolved that the General Manager be asked to consider running the two freight trains at suitable times and then accommodate passengers by putting carriages on each service and running them as mixed trains. Again the idea was considered uneconomic and was soon quashed.

In the early months of 1866, Messrs Garrett & Sons of Aldeburgh had experienced flooding on their property near Snape station and in April complained to GER headquarters of the bad condition of the sluice passing under the railway. The Engineer was asked to investigate and on examination found the culvert under the line was formed of simple wooden trunking as a continuation of an open ditch, which existed before the railway was constructed. Garrett required the railway company to fix a flap at one end to prevent the water back flowing through the gulley and thus obviate the flooding. Davis, the Engineer, was not happy with the suggestion, as providing the flap would only divert water back to flood neighbouring property, whose owners would then complain. The matter was discussed at the Traffic Committee meeting on 25th April, 1866 and passed to Maynard for further action. The solution finally agreed was to dig another minor channel to remove the excess of water.

On 7th November, 1866 the Directors were surprised to learn that the GER goods shed at Snape had been sold by Sir Samuel Morton Peto to Newson Garrett in 1863, as part of surplus lands of the former East Suffolk Railway. The sale was effected four years after the shed was built by Peto, and despite attempts to reclaim the building, Newson Garrett maintained his claim to the property and refused to enter into negotiation with either Peto or the GER. The matter was passed to the Traffic Committee for settlement and they requested Messrs Shaw and Dobbin, the solicitors to investigate. They in turn found that Peto had no right to sell the land or goods shed after the takeover of the ESR and creation of the GER, and Garrett was forced to hand both shed and land back to the railway company.

Early in March 1868 complaints were made regarding the poor condition of the fencing at Snape station. The matter was passed to Shaw, who duly reported on 1st April that there was considerable doubt as to the liability of the GER to repair the fence, but the understanding was to get the fence repaired and then ask the parish to take over maintenance. Dobbin confirmed the fence had been repaired and the parish had agreed to accept responsibility for future maintenance and repairs. In the meantime the branch was publicised in a most curious way for an advertisement appeared in the local press advising the sale of the wrecked brigantine *Wallace* as timber, which was lying at Snape 'convenient for railway and other cartage'.

Despite the ruling made in 1866, Garrett again complained on 10th June, 1868 that the railway company had taken some of his land, which was now occupied by the goods shed and cattle pens. On 24th June the letter was lodged with the GER Law Clerk who promised to look into the question. The matter was subsequently referred to Shaw, who asked the traffic superintendent and the goods manager for their comments. Both officers were highly vexed by Garrett's continual complaining and announced on 12th August, 1868 they considered it desirable to close the station and withdraw the train service from the branch. The solicitor, however, advised that the company was precluded from taking such action in consequence of the agreement made between Garrett and Sir Samuel Morton Peto when the line was built, and the subsequent agreement with the GER. Once again the Law Clerk was asked to investigate a way round the impasse. Frustrated by lack of progress, Garrett then disputed rental payments in September 1869. The subject remained dormant for the next two years and it was not until 4th July, 1871 that the Legal and Parliamentary Committee were advised that the GER Company had indeed encroached upon Garrett's land. He was under no obligation to sell or let the portion of land to the company and was perfectly at liberty by law to take possession of the goods shed and other buildings erected on the site. He was also entitled to withhold rent for other company land he occupied until the question was settled. By 8th

November wiser counsels prevailed and in an effort to end the dispute, Garrett suggested he would allow the GER Company to occupy the land on which the buildings were erected for an annual rental of £1, provided 'no coals or goods shall be run on the line in opposition to his trade there'. The goods manager thought selling the land or accepting the long-term lease for rental of £1 per annum was the best way of settling the affair but was unhappy with Garrett's imposition refusing other traders access to the line. William Birt, the General Manager, agreed and said if the lease was not taken the company should shut the line or move the station to another site. After further discussion it was agreed to lease the land at a perpetual rate of £1 per annum, but no restriction would be made on the use of the line or conveyance of other traders merchandise and Garrett was advised accordingly.

In the autumn of 1871 the traffic superintendent had urged the installation of the block telegraph on the East Suffolk line between Ipswich and Saxmundham to obviate pathing problems with express services, especially to Aldeburgh, which were delayed by slower Parliamentary services. The GER Traffic Committee raised the subject at their meeting on 12th March, 1872, when it was estimated the cost of Tyer's telegraph, provision of new signal boxes and signals including an installation at Snape Junction, would be £800. The improved arrangements would involve additional cost of wages to signalmen estimated at £8 per week or £400 per annum. The matter was placed in abeyance for almost a year before being passed to the Board to sanction on 26th February, 1873.

Having provided a signal box at Snape Junction to control traffic on the main line and access to and from the branch, the GER traffic superintendent requested the provision of a cottage for the signalman based at the isolated location. The Way and Works Committee invited tenders and on 14th January, 1874 authorized the provision of the cottage at an estimated cost of £220. The contract was duly awarded to G. Carter on 11th February after he had tendered at £199. The following month the traffic superintendent advised the points and signals at the junction were still not interlocked but it was a further eight years before any work was carried out.

On 14th June, 1876 a lad shepherd inadvertently left open one of the gates of an occupational crossing on the branch, after driving a flock of sheep into the adjacent field. He then left the animals unattended so that when the branch goods train arrived the engine ran into the flock and killed one of the beasts. The farmer attempted to claim compensation but withdrew his claim on being advised the gate was left open allowing access to the railway.

During an inspection of their system on 1st and 2nd October, 1878, the GER Directors visited the Snape branch and on arrival at the terminus had a short meeting with Newson Garrett. They negotiated an agreement over the disputed land used by the company and enquired of station master George Maskell the state of traffic. At the first meeting of the Traffic Committee after the visit, it was resolved to pay Garrett £50 for the use of the land and include the transfer of property in the new Bill being presented to Parliament. The Directors were evidently not satisfied with traffic levels for they asked for a return of all traffic, other than Garrett's, for the previous 12 months.

Snape goods station and maltings c.1910, viewed from the Tunstall to Snape road, with the goods shed in the foreground and behind that the station master's house.

Early in 1882 a special committee of the Traffic Committee sanctioned the allocation of £20,000 towards expenditure for the interlocking of signals at stations on the East Suffolk line. At that time Robertson, the GER traffic superintendent, was asking for interlocking of signals and points at Snape Junction as well as Darsham, Tivetshall, Needham and several other places. The work forming part of a package costing £5,620 was authorized on 16th May, 1882. In the same year Newson Garrett's son, George Herbert, was appointed Manager at the maltings, where output was continuing to grow and another building was constructed in 1885. On 30th December, 1884 the GER Way and Works Committee agreed to the installation of a speaking telegraph linking Ipswich and Beccles, via intermediate signal boxes at a cost of £350.

The Regulation of Railways Act 1889 amongst other things enforced major railway companies to adopt block working on all except single lines where the Train Staff without Ticket and One Engine in Steam systems existed. On the GER the Snape branch was one of the few lines without block working. When initially inspected the route had been passed for passenger train working, but only freight trains had ever operated. As only goods traffic would continue to be handled the GER authorities decided on 3rd December, 1889 to withdraw the existing Train Staff and Ticket method of working and thus obviate the necessity of upgrading the line to full block working. In accordance with procedures, the company was required to confirm to the BOT within two years the method of working the branch, and the GER Secretary on 25th January, 1892 duly forwarded the certificate showing the method of working to be adopted on the Snape branch. The document recorded that only One Engine in Steam or two or more coupled together would be allowed on the single line at one and the same time with the single line Train Staff carried on the locomotive. On receipt of the correspondence the following day, the certificate was passed to General C.S. Hutchinson for comment. The inspector was satisfied with the arrangements, which he considered were intended to supersede the existing arrangements. After commenting that he 'believed the Snape branch was not now used for passenger traffic', he recommended adoption of the new method of working, which was introduced almost immediately.

Newson Garrett passed away at the age of 81 in 1893, after dominating affairs around Snape Bridge and the upper reaches of the River Alde for over 50 years. The malting business was divided equally among his children. It was soon after that the very last malt house, known as the New House, was erected. At that time the maltings had approximately seven acres of floor space with employment for 30 men.

Adverse weather affected the branch when a severe blizzard and driving winds on 14th February, 1900 caused snowdrifts to block the line in several places especially in the cutting near Snape Junction. The branch was of low priority for snow clearance and it was three days before permanent way staff managed to clear the line for goods train services to resume.

On 23rd December, 1907, the GER Secretary advised the BOT that the Snape branch line, which was passed for passenger train working, was now only being worked as a goods line. The company therefore intended to provide signalling only at Snape Junction where the branch joined the main line, and which was

GER 'Y14' class 0-6-0 tender locomotive No. 923 departs from Snape over the River Alde underbridge with a train formed of a GER 20 tons goods brakevan and Midland Railway open wagon c.1910.

already interlocked. The following day the letter was passed to Colonel P.G. Von Donop who after consideration asked the company to submit a plan showing the signalling arrangements at the junction. He further commented, 'subject to the arrangements being satisfactory, the Board of Trade cannot as far as I am aware raise any objections to the company's proposals'. The drawing dated 13th January, 1908 was duly submitted to Von Donop five days later. On 21st January he expressed his opinion that the arrangements were satisfactory and commented, 'an inspection hardly seems necessary'. The GER was advised of the recommendation the following day. As a result of the new arrangements all signalling was removed at Snape.

In 1910 George Garrett handed over the day-to-day management of Snape maltings to Maurice Cowell, a grandson of Newson Garrett, but few changes were made. Later in the year on 9th December, 1910, heavy rainfall caused extensive flooding in parts of East Anglia. Delays occurred to train services on the Framlingham branch and the Waveney Valley line but the Snape goods line suffered more extensive flooding with the track under water as the Alde burst its banks. Ballast was washed away and the permanent way damaged to the extent that train services were suspended until remedial repairs were carried out. Flooding again closed the branch on 26th August, 1912 after heavy rainfall deluged the area. Like the neighbouring Framlingham branch, which was also affected, the Snape branch was not reopened until 27th August.

The outbreak of World War I on 4th August, 1914 found the GER, with other railway companies, under Government control. Train services continued to run to pre-war timetables and goods traffic gradually increased as farmers and growers were urged to increase production of grain, vegetables and root crops, to make up for the loss of imported foods caused by enemy action against shipping. The additional traffic was noticeable on the Snape branch for there was increasing difficulty delivering barley via coastal ports and the Alde to the maltings. Farmers and growers rallying to the call arranged for the barley to be sent by rail and occasionally an additional train ran across the branch to maintain the output at the maltings. Equally the malt was dispatched via the branch to various breweries throughout London and East Anglia. In the meantime Maurice Cowell had left the maltings to enlist in the Army, where he attained the rank of Major but was unfortunately killed in 1916. After this devastating loss George Garrett returned to take over the running of the establishment.

The strain of the war years taxed the resources of the railways and in December 1916, the Railway Executive Committee issued an ultimatum, to the effect that they would only continue if drastic reductions were made to ordinary services. Locomotive power was short, through lack of coal supplies, and the Lloyd George Coalition agreed to the reduction of passenger services from 1st January, 1917 to release additional power for freight and military services. The guarantee of motive power to the Snape branch ensured the continuing dispatch of malt by rail to the London breweries but by March the German submarine stranglehold on shipping in the North Sea forced the Government Wheat Committee to start taking 'Ale Barley' for malting. Later in the same year the Ministry of Food ordered Snape to cease malting and train services on the branch were suspended. The line lay disused for a few weeks until a contract was obtained from the Grain Committee for wheat to be brought to Snape by rail and barge for storage but this only lasted for two months. At the start of the barley season in October the maltings and branch lay dormant awaiting receipt of the necessary trading licence. Fortunately this was received in November 1917, but output was only two-sevenths of pre-war production, with George Garrett stating he had not seen such a poor quality of barley in the area. Matters soon improved and outgoing traffic receipts were enhanced by the dispatch of hay used as fodder and bedding by the many military establishments in East Anglia and the Home Counties, some of the hay being cut from the railway embankments and cuttings on the branch.

During 1918 George Garrett merged the Snape establishment with the malting company of S. Swonnell & Sons Limited of Oulton Broad, Lowestoft. The company had resulted from a merger in 1898 between George Swonnell, a maltster of Nine Elms, Battersea, London and Tomkins, Courage and Cracknell and moved to Oulton Broad in 1902. George Garrett had been purchasing the shares of this competitor since 1892 and also shares in such dubious concerns as the United Railway of Havana and the Central Argentine Railway. He was in fact Chairman of Swonnell's until 1929. The maltings at Oulton Broad and Snape were, however, run quite separately. The new company pledged its continued reliance on rail transport for the receipt of barley and coal and coke and dispatch of malt to the breweries. As a result of the increase in traffic during the war years very little maintenance was carried out on the permanent way across the branch and at Snape. Due to the limited accommodation at Snape, the GE company used the siding belonging to Swonnell and Sons Limited to shunt wagons, as their own siding was in need of urgent repairs. Early in 1919 Swonnell's wrote to the GER Board asking the company to undertake repairs to its private sidings as well as the railway-owned siding. At the same time it was suggested the wagon turntable, which was considered life expired, be renewed at cost to Swonnell. The engineer reported to the Traffic Committee that he estimated the cost of repairs to the sidings at £590 and renewal of the turntable at £440. The work was authorized on 6th February, 1919 with the GER portion agreed at £295.

The general feeling of elation at the cessation of hostilities were shattered by a railway strike which halted services on the branch and indeed surrounding branches and main lines from 26th September to 8th October, 1919. Two years later the miners' strike affected coal supplies, and although services on the Snape branch were not suspended, sudden cancellations were made on a number of occasions. This industrial action began the decline in railway goods services. Farmers and growers realised that with improving roads, commodities could be conveyed by motor lorry, utilising vehicles purchased second-hand or surplus from the army, thus permitting short haul journeys to be made to Snape at cheaper rates than charged by the GER. The primitive commercial vehicles of the day were not, however, capable of continuous long hauls and the middle and long distance consignments remained safely in the hands of the railway company.

As a result of the 1921 Railways Act, from 1st January, 1923 the GER was amalgamated with the Great Northern, Great Central, North Eastern and several smaller railways to form the London & North Eastern Railway. The new owner made few initial changes to the Snape branch, save that some of the locomotives working the line soon appeared with the legend 'LNER' on the tender sides, whilst railway-owned wagons showed the ownership of their new company. Industrial action again affected affairs when a seven-day railway strike from 20th January, 1924 brought a further decline in traffic receipts. Industrial unrest also affected the maltings the following year, when on 30th October the 24 maltsters gave 14 days' notice to cease work. The following day Mr Silvester, the Manager, met the men in his office to hear of their demands for a 5s. 0d. per week rise instead of the 10s. 0d. bonus. They also wanted £20 payment for every shipment of malt handled and topped it up with a demand for two pints of beer per day. The maltsters also asked for a reduction in the working day, which was then from 5 am to 5 pm. Silvester agreed to a 10-hour day from 5 am to 3 pm on condition that they stayed later, if required, to finish malt production. He could not, however, offer an advance in wages or pay more for each shipment of malt. The maltsters were not satisfied and several of the younger employees advocated complete withdrawal of labour as a demand for increased wages. Some of the older men were not in favour of stopping work and were subsequently threatened with violence. In this backwater of Suffolk, such flexing of muscles by workers was unheard of, and matters came to a head when it was announced Swonnell's would close down the maltings in the event of any action. On 4th November, 1925 the police were drafted in to maintain the peace, and thereafter a satisfactory solution to the benefit of both parties was quickly reached. During the upheaval, train services were suspended on a number of days because of lack of traffic, whilst the local railwaymen working the branch wholeheartedly supported the staff at the maltings. The following year services were once again disrupted by the General Strike in early May 1926. Railway union members withdrew their labour in support of the miners and subsequently train services could not be guaranteed. On several occasions the Snape branch service was suspended, but after a week or so regular railwaymen returned to work and trains again ran on the Suffolk goods line. The impact of the continuing miners' strike meant coal stocks were low, and the LNER management decided to reduce services to conserve their coal supplies. From 31st May, 1926 revised timetables were introduced affecting mainly the passenger services, but on a number of occasions during this period the Snape branch trip was cancelled at short notice or covered by the Framlingham branch engine. After the upheaval of 1925 the staff at Snape maltings continued to work.

Snow again blocked the branch in December 1927, falling on Christmas Day evening. As there was no traffic for two days, no snow clearance was attempted until all the main line and passenger branches in the area were cleared. It was thus four days before the branch was again open for traffic.

Over the years traders had been complaining of late arrival of consignments at Snape and also of delays to outward-bound goods. The local goods manager was delegated to investigate and on 19th July, 1929, the Divisional General Manager (Southern Area) submitted a report to the Traffic Committee. The matter was discussed at their meeting on 25th July when it was revealed the accommodation for dealing with the branch goods traffic was totally inadequate and wagons were often being held back at other places until they could be accepted at Snape. Traders had threatened to divert traffic to road transport unless improvements were effected. The existing sidings could accommodate 40 wagons with cart access available to 32 wagons. To obviate the problem it was proposed to increase the space behind the existing siding and make up the ground to provide better facilities for the movement of traders vehicles. The scheme, providing additional siding space for seven wagons, of which five would have cart access, was estimated to cost £756 including £120 for a small amount of land. Adoption was expected to show a saving in engine shunting time, estimated at £33 per annum and the Traffic Committee and Works Committee both agreed the expenditure. At the end of the same year the LNER purchased 21 poles of land from Swonnell & Sons, later known as Swonnell & Sons Limited (London), for the princely sum of £21 to enable the work to commence.

From then until the outbreak of World War II goods traffic continued to be conveyed by the one freight train in each direction on weekdays only. In the late 1920s sugar beet cultivation had been introduced into the area and during winter months a reasonable tonnage was conveyed from Snape to the beet factories at Ipswich, Bury St Edmunds and Cantley, augmenting the receipts already earned from the barley and malt traffic. The branch, however, did not have the monopoly for Snape maltings received, on average, one barge of barley and dispatched the same vessel with bagged malt per month, although at the beginning of the malting season one or two additional craft tied up at the quay. G.F. Sully operated the barges during this period. Motor lorries also started regularly to convey local traffic.

Prior to the outbreak of hostilities on 3rd September, 1939 the LNER, together with all other major railway companies, came under the control of the Railway Executive Committee. The Snape branch was in a vulnerable position near a coastal inlet, which might at any time be infiltrated by enemy troops and the area was designated a restricted zone. The sailing barge traffic up the River Alde was stopped, and all barley and coal and coke transferred to rail. During the war Snape was scheduled as a Defence Area because of it proximity to the coast and some children were evacuated from the locality. When there was threat of Luftwaffe air attacks, the siren mounted on the maltings advised local people to take cover and although several bombs fell in the area, none affected the branch railway. As a precaution against air raids, especially at night or during fog or falling snow, staff utilised shielded hand lamps to attend to train and shunting duties. In addition coastal defence armoured trains patrolled the various branches in East Suffolk between June 1940 and July 1943, during which time the Snape branch was regularly covered, initially by train D and then by train C. After returning from patrols in Cornwall train D, by now based at Mistley, resumed its activities on Essex and Suffolk branch lines until disbanded in July 1943. The agricultural nature of the freight handled was of the utmost importance in the war years as the vital provisions of home grown food, vegetables, grain and sugar beet were dispatched and conveyed to markets and the Snape branch saw its share of increased traffic.

The LNER, like other railway companies, resumed peacetime activities with run-down and life-expired rolling stock and equipment. Questions were raised in Parliament regarding the deteriorating services and the poor condition of rolling stock, which had received minimal maintenance during the hostilities. The Snape branch was no exception and on occasions the service was cancelled through lack of locomotive power available at Ipswich depot or insufficient wagons to handle the traffic. Further disruption came in the early months of 1947 when heavy snowfalls blocked the line and access roads to Snape. The Ipswich-based snowplough was initially engaged clearing the main lines and passenger carrying branches in East Suffolk before attention was turned to the line to Snape, and the goods branch was low on the list of priorities. Later as petrol rationing eased, farmers and growers in the area transferred much of the barley traffic to road haulage and indeed outgoing malt to local breweries was sent by the same method, with a resultant loss of trade to the railway.

The nationalisation of the railways from 1st January, 1948 brought few alterations to the Snape branch, which retained its GER/LNER atmosphere until closure. The ubiquitous 'J15' class 0-6-0 locomotives still worked the trip to the maltings and back but gradually lost their NE or LNER identity from the tender sides, to be replaced by the legend 'BRITISH RAILWAYS'. Wagons and goods brake vans were progressively painted in the new corporate BR identity. Within a month of assuming control British Railways took over a former War Department store at Snape, free of charge, to use as a sack store.

During and after World War II until 1948, rubble from blitzed buildings was sent down from London to Snape Bridge, initially for gun site bases and later for land reclamation. Often two trains ran each weekday being worked as 'bonus' freight trains with crews being paid extra for getting from Ipswich to Snape and back as quickly as possible. Later as clearance progressed, the working was reduced to one train and then ceased altogether. The normal branch freight services were also converted to 'bonus' runs with no fixed intermediate timings, the train running as quickly as possible from Ipswich to Saxmundham and Snape and return by control instructions, being pathed between the mandatory timetabled services over the East Suffolk main line. Over the years the malting business had grown resulting in the construction of the final building in the complex, that of a grain store in 1952. This small extension was built on the front facade behind the public house, alongside a section built in 1885. By the early 1950s Swonnell's, however, had ceased importing barley and exporting malt by rail, having transferred this to road transport and the branch train then only conveyed coal and coke for the maltings, often running only once a week. In June 1956 the railway authorities entered into an agreement with S. Swonnell & Sons Limited of Saxmundham to construct flood barriers and raise the level of the railway embankment near the terminus to prevent water inundating the surrounding property during winter months.

In the 1950s enthusiast interest in railways increased considerably and on 30th September, 1956, the first passenger train ventured on to the goods-only Snape branch. The Railway Enthusiasts' Club 'Suffolk Venturer' Railtour, formed of five Gresley corridor coaches in carmine and cream livery, hauled by

At certain times and especially after World War II, Ipswich shed was unable to provide a 'J15' class 0-6-0 tender locomotive for the Snape goods train. When this occurred, a 'J17' class 0-6-0 tender engine usually deputised but because of weight restriction was unable to work across the branch. Any wagons for Snape were left in the up reception siding at Snape Junction and arrangements were made for the Framlingham branch locomotive to run to Snape Junction to take the wagons to the Snape and return with any loaded or empty wagons to Wickham Market. As the locomotive allocated to work the Framlingham branch was normally an 'F3' class 2-4-2 tank locomotive with a route availability category of RA3, special dispensation was given for the class to work across the branch. Here 'F3' No. 7143 complete with a stopping passenger train headcode and with driver Bloom looking out of the cab, departs from Snape with the branch freight comprised of loaded vans of malt. The previous day the same engine had deputised for a failed 'B12/3' class 4-6-0 tender locomotive on a Liverpool Street to Yarmouth express, taking over from the failed engine at Wickham Market.

The late Dr I.C. Allen

'E4' class 2-4-0 tender locomotive No. 62797, had earlier visited the Bentley to Hadleigh branch and run short of steam on the return working near Capel. After working down from Snape Junction the train was prevented from fully entering the sidings at Snape because both lines were partially blocked by wagons. Enthusiasts descended from the train to take photographs before No. 62797 propelled the formation back to the junction. Unfortunately the train was halted on the 1 in 98/66 rising gradient on the approach to Snape Junction to allow the up Halesworth milk train to pass. Restarting the train proved too much for the ailing 'E4' and the locomotive stalled on the bank, again short of steam. The decision was taken to send for assistance, which finally arrived in the form of 'J15' class 0-6-0 tender locomotive No. 65447. This easily hauled the five coaches and its locomotive back on the East Suffolk main line. The 'J15' then piloted the train forward from Snape Junction. The special also visited the Wensum Valley line and the Eye branch.

As world trade developed it became apparent that locally grown barley could not support the huge maltings at Snape, and cheaper imported barley was brought in by road and by sailing barges from London Docks. Some imported coal and coke for the malt drying kilns was also transported by road and barge, and tonnages conveyed by rail began to decline. By the late 1950s the maltings at Snape were becoming outdated and registered to most as a charming piece of Victorian enterprise, far removed from the developing modern industry in Britain. Although sugar beet was conveyed in season, the branch traffic for the maltings continued to dwindle and often the trip working between Snape Junction and Snape was cancelled. Swonnell's would not guarantee to send traffic by train and advised local railway officers they would elect to use the cheapest transport, which in most cases was not by British Railways. Another factor also entered the equation, for when the local civil engineer investigated the infrastructure of the branch it became all too apparent a considerable amount of money would be required to rebuild the timber bridges on the line. The ageing 'J15' class 0-6-0 tender locomotives, which had valiantly worked the branch for over 60 years, were almost life expired. Many were being scrapped along with other steam locomotives, as the British Railways modernisation programme for traction was introduced. Unfortunately for the Snape branch, no new main line diesel locomotive was light enough to run across the branch as a ready replacement for the 'J15' class; the British Thomson Houston/Paxman type 800 hp Bo-Bo locomotives had been initially considered. The only alternative was a diesel-mechanical shunting locomotive, but to operate one of these on the daily goods trip with its maximum speed of 15 mph along the East Suffolk main line was tantamount to major operating disruption of the timetable. The outcome of the situation was inevitable and notices were duly posted advising the branch was to be closed on and from 7th March, 1960. In the final months of operation trains only served the branch on an as and when required basis. Often a week would pass without a train arriving at or departing from Snape and the last train actually ran on Friday 4th March with 'J15' class No. 65389 running light to Snape with a brake van before clearing the yard of six open wagons and a covered van. The formation then returned to Snape Junction and on to Ipswich.

When the Railway Enthusiasts' Club special train arrived at Snape on 30th September, 1956, it was not possible for the engine and five coaches to be accommodated in either siding as both were occupied by wagons. Here 'E4' class 2-4-0 tender locomotive No. 62797 stands with her train on the goods shed loop as participants take photographs and inspect the yard.

The late B.D.J. Walsh

'E4' class 2-4-0 No. 62797, allocated to Lowestoft shed, stands at Snape with the Railway Enthusiast's railtour train on 30th September, 1956. *Hugh Davies*

HISTORY OF THE LINE

The only passenger train to run to Snape was the Railway Enthusiasts' Club 'Suffolk Venturer' railtour on Sunday 30th September, 1956. Formed of five ex-LNER Gresley corridor coaches the train was hauled by 'E4' class 2-4-0 tender locomotive No. 62797. The special had earlier visited the Hadleigh branch, where the locomotive ran short of steam. After visiting Snape the engine again ran short of steam on the return working whilst propelling the coaches up the gradient to Snape Junction and assistance had to be obtained to pull the train clear of the branch. Here No. 62797 and her train stands just short of the junction whilst waiting the arrival of the assisting engine, class 'J15' No. 65447.
The late Dr I.C. Allen

The reason for stopping the Railway Enthusiasts' Club railtour train on the rising 1 in 66 gradient approaching Snape Junction on 30th September, 1956, was to allow the Halesworth milk train to pass *en route* to Ipswich. Here 'L1 class' 2-6-4 tank locomotive No. 67775 hurries the train, formed of a van and milk tanks, past the junction.
The late B.D.J. Walsh

The branch up home signal is cleared as 'J15' class 0-6-0 No. 65447 sets to work pulling the stranded Railway Enthusiasts' Club 'Suffolk Venturer' special train off the Snape branch on 30th September, 1956. The line can be seen at a lower level to the right. *The late Dr I.C. Allen*

The steep climb from the Snape branch to the East Suffolk main line is evident as 'J15' class 0-6-0 tender locomotive No. 65447 assists the Railway Enthusiasts' Club tour train on to the up main at Snape Junction on 30th September, 1956. 'E4' class 2-4-0 No. 62797 makes a valiant effort banking at the rear of the five-coach formation. *The late B.D.J. Walsh*

After the withdrawal of services the track remained *in situ* for several months gradually succumbing to a growth of weeds and small bushes. Early in 1961 contractors arrived to lift the rails and sleepers, working from the junction back to the terminus. Rails were cut into short lengths and loaded on to lorries, which carted the material away from site via the several occupational crossings along the line. The station house and associated 1 acre 1 rod and 35 poles of land were sold to S. Swonnell & Son Limited for £1,500 on 3rd August, 1961. The following year on 8th March, 1962, 3.494 acres of the former trackbed was sold to Mrs K. Hurren, whilst a section comprising 2.75 acres near the former junction was sold to W.F. Turner for £82, provided he maintained the boundary fence with the East Suffolk main line. Another 1.7 acres of the former goods branch was sold for £42 to H.R. Bond on 21st October, 1964, whilst the final five acres was disposed of for £925 on 4th November, 1964.

S. Swonnell & Sons went into voluntary liquidation in 1965 and Snape Maltings were closed when 42 men lost their employment. Competition from more modern and economic methods used elsewhere made their increasingly costly operation unviable. Major breweries were purchasing their own maltings in order to secure their own supplies of raw material. The massive capital investments to ensure modern production methods brought the demise of the under-capitalised family-owned malting businesses, and Swonnell's was one of many that succumbed. George Gooderham (Investments) Limited bought the malting complex in 1965 before the buildings were vandalised and dereliction set in. The Gooderham family business had developed into Gooderham and Hayward animal food compounds, working from a mill located alongside Marlesford station on the neighbouring Framlingham branch. In 1966/7 Derek Sugden of Ove Arup Partnership converted one of the maltings, New House, as a concert hall for the Aldeburgh Festival, which was formally opened by Her Majesty Queen Elizabeth II in 1967. Unfortunately fire destroyed the first conversion but the building was re-restored in 1969/70 and today is famed worldwide for the marvellous acoustics, which enhance the performers at the various concerts held throughout the year. The remaining sections of the former industrial complex have been converted to studios and quality retail outlets, whilst the Plough and Sail public house continues to provide sustenance to the passer-by.

Today there are few signs of the former Snape branch. At the site of Snape Junction the railway boundary fence crosses the former trackbed. Beyond the fence the path of the line through the shallow cutting is discernible, whilst hedgerows mark the boundary of railway where the line passed through pasture. Short embankments still mark the path of the trackbed on either side of the former timber bridges across streams and the River Alde before arrival at Snape where the station house is now a private residence. Opposite the house are the remains of the former goods shed office, whilst an ex-GER goods van body stands isolated from track in the former goods yard.

Snape goods station site facing towards the maltings in 1998. *Author*

Snape station master's house, now a private dwelling, in 1998. *Author*

The remains of former GER covered van No. 6102 on the site of Snape goods yard in 1998.
Author

Above left: View from the archway of the maltings to the former Snape station site in 1998.
Author

Above right: The road frontage of Snape maltings in 1998. The slight curve was attributed to Newson Garrett marking out the lineage with his walking stick. In the industrial heyday a siding ran along the front of the building so that barley could be offloaded from wagons and hoisted into the upper rooms via the lucams, whilst loaded sacks of malt were lowered into rail vehicles for onward transit to breweries in London and East Anglia. *Author*

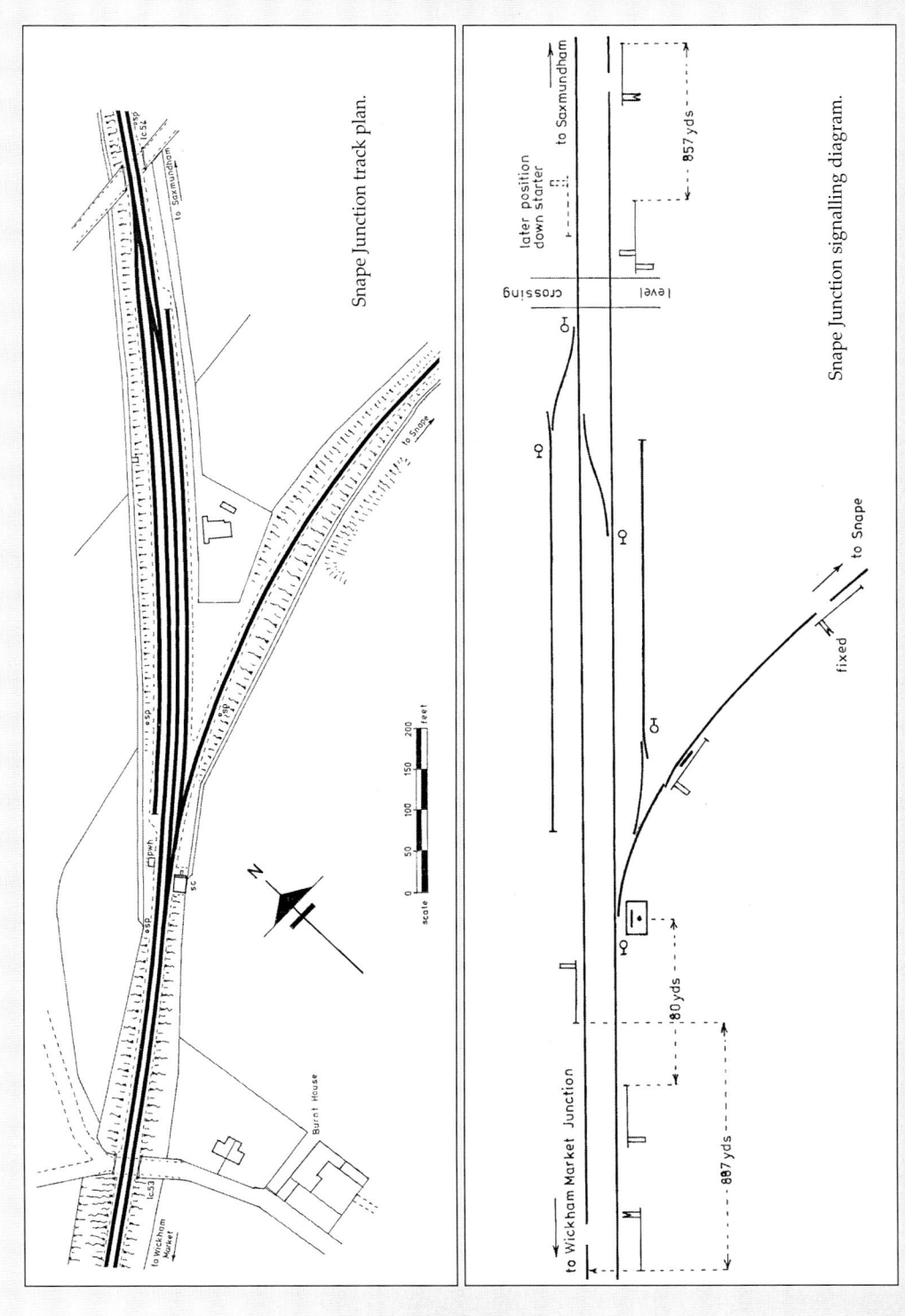

Chapter Two

The Route Described

The Snape goods branch formed a trailing connection with the up East Suffolk main line at Snape Junction, 88 miles 08 chains from Liverpool Street, and just north of Burnt House level crossing, No. 53 at 88 miles 03 chains. To facilitate down trains shunting on to the branch, a trailing crossover was provided between the up and down main lines just south of Farnham/Snape level crossing No. 54, at 88 miles 23 chains. Reception sidings were provided on both up and down sides of the line entered by trailing points in the direction of travel, the down side being 750 feet in length whilst the up side was 640 feet long. Both could accommodate a train of 27 wagons. All signals and points at the junction were controlled by Snape Junction signal box equipped with a 22 lever frame. Later civil engineering diagrams showed Snape Junction as 88 miles 17 chains but for sake of clarity the Great Eastern mileages are quoted herein.

The single line Snape branch curved away from the main line on a 16 chain radius right-hand curve, falling initially at 1 in 249 past the branch up home signal located on the up side of the line, and continuing at 1 in 66 through a shallow cutting. The railway then followed a straight course to the south-east bisecting Botany Wood footpath crossing No. 1, at 88 miles 24 chains, and passing the associated Botany Wood and Botany Cottage to the north of the line. The gradient continued to fall at 1 in 98 as the railway ran across a shallow embankment. The line then started to climb at 1 in 677 as the branch passed Snape Junction branch up distant signal, located on the south side of the line, before bisecting occupational crossing No. 2 at 88 miles 48 chains. Beyond the crossing the railway following a 40 chains radius right-hand curve, passing in later years a pre-cast concrete permanent way hut on the up side of the line, before bisecting Groom's level crossing, No. 3 at 88 miles 57 chains. Immediately after the crossing the railway spanned a minor stream and an area liable to flooding on Groom's underbridge, No. 1107 at 88 miles 61 chains. The branch then curved across a shallow embankment to continue a straight course over footpath crossing No. 4, at 88 miles 76 chains, and then over Stream underbridge No. 1108 at 89 miles 0 chains. Snape Maltings were prominent on the skyline as the branch continued its straight course, falling initially at 1 in 320 and then climbing at 1 in 440 through a minor cutting and over footpath crossing No. 5 at 89 miles 21 chains. Beyond the crossing the line ran over a short embankment before crossing the tidal River Alde, on Snape River underbridge No. 1109 at 89 miles 28 chains. Immediately beyond the seven-span structure the line fell at 1 in 125, passing over footpath crossing No. 6 at 89 miles 29 chains and then a shallow embankment, to enter Snape goods station, 89 miles 40 chains from Liverpool Street and 1 miles 32 chains from Snape Junction, on a 1 in 408 rising gradient and 18 chains radius left-hand curve.

The track layout at Snape consisted of the locally known shed road to the south of the layout, which served the goods shed and a 660 ft-long reception

In the event of the Ipswich to Saxmundham and Snape goods train being allocated anything other than a 'J15' class 0-6-0 tender locomotive, or cancellation of the service, arrangements were made for the locomotive working the Framlingham branch to run from Wickham Market to Snape and back to pick up any outgoing wagons. Here 'J15' No. 65478 propels its brake van past Snape Junction signal box on the down main line before crossing over to the up main line and then reversing down the branch. *The late Dr I.C. Allen*

Permanent way renewals are in progress at Snape Junction as 'J15' class No. 65389 waits at the up branch home signal with the Snape goods. *Dr J. Westall/A. Vaughan Collection*

loop siding, both of which terminated one chain beyond railway property on a wagon turntable. The entry points to the loop were 1 mile 23 chains from Snape Junction at 89 miles 31 chains. At the east end of the railway property on the north side of the reception loop was the station house, with its two tall chimneystacks and hipped roof. The building, complete with a passenger booking hall, although it never served as such, was constructed in a similar style to station houses on the East Suffolk main line and Framlingham and Aldeburgh branches. In 1913 James Henry Lewis Crosby the station master occupied the station, paying an annual rent of £14 for station and garden but by 1924 Henry Waller was paying £16. Immediately opposite the station house on the south side of the shed road was the goods shed and associated office. The building fell into disrepair and was pulled down in February and March 1957, leaving only the small office section standing. At one time a 170 ft-long siding with trailing connection for down trains ran to the south of the shed siding. The points and signals at Snape were originally controlled from a small signal hut but in 1891 a small ground level signal box was provided, located at the west end of the yard to the north of the points. A signal post bearing signal arms for each direction of travel also stood alongside the loop line at the west end of the platform, but this was removed in 1908. After the abolition of the signal box in 1943 the points were operated by a ground frame but in 1946 they were converted to hand operation.

Beyond the station house and railway boundary, the two tracks continued over the public road linking Snape and Tunstall, later B1069 by level crossing No. 7, at 89 miles 40 chains, to converge on to the 13 feet 6 inches-diameter wagon turntable located immediately in front of the impressive arched entrance to the maltings, constructed in 1859, and leading to the inner courtyard of the premises. The turntable served sidings running at right angles to the entrance siding, leading in each direction, both fronting onto the long line of buildings and offices, which curved slightly on its western face between railway and river. The curving frontage of the maltings was stated to have been established when Newson Garrett marked out the front line of the buildings with a walking stick. Several of the facades had lucams used for hoisting the sacks of barley to the tops of the buildings and conversely loading up railway wagons with sacks of malt. Having reached the end of the buildings the siding to the north of the turntable divided into three roads, all of which reached the quayside, enabling goods to be transferred to and from the sailing barges. One of these sidings was provided with a 1 ton 10 cwt-capacity fixed crane to assist loading and unloading. Another of the sidings passed close to the back door of the Plough and Sail public house.

The main siding from the turntable passed through the curved arched entrance, with its 1859 dated and initialled keystone, and served a long loading platform with corrugated iron canopy, located to the south of the line, which was used for offloading coal and coke traffic. This siding continued to a second wagon turntable in the centre of the malthouse complex and this had three sidings running from it. The main siding ran in a northerly direction, parallel with the sidings on the exterior of the maltings and passed between two rows of malt houses. This siding, which extended to serve the quay, had two trailing connections, one running along the north side of the New House, which is now

The Snape branch swung away from Snape Junction to the east on a 16 chain radius right-hand curve on a falling 1 in 249/66 gradient past Botany Wood before following a straight course past Snape Junction up fixed distant signal, which can be seen in the background. The formation of the railway at this point was very wide, although double track was never planned or installed.
The late B.D.J. Walsh

'J15' class 0-6-0 No. 65430 hauls the branch train away from Snape Junction and down the line towards Snape. The branch was built on a slight embankment above the flood plain.
The late Dr I.C. Allen

Although officially limited to a speed limit of 15 mph on the branch, train crews working the 'bonus' goods which served Snape were always in a hurry to get back to Ipswich and the speed restriction was often ignored. The footplate crew of 'J15' 0-6-0 No. 65430 appear to taken such action and have just shut off steam as the lightweight train of a five-plank open wagon and brake van begins the climb to Snape Junction. *The late Dr I.C. Allen*

The single track Snape branch facing towards Snape Junction with occupational crossing No. 2, at 88 miles 48 chains, in the foreground and beyond the crossing the up branch distant signal. Note the lineside fencing formed of old sleepers with wire stranding and the ash and clinker ballast of the permanent way. *The late B.D.J. Walsh*

A straight section of the Snape branch looking towards Snape Junction with Stream underbridge No. 1108 in the foreground and beyond that occupational crossing No 4 at 88 miles 76 chains.
The late B.D.J. Walsh

The straight section of line on the approach to Snape with occupational crossing No. 5 at 89 miles 21 chains from Liverpool Street in the foreground. The track is formed of 30 ft length bullhead rails, whilst in the background wagons can be seen stabled in the goods yard.
The late B.D.J. Walsh

Snape River underbridge No. 1109, spanning the River Alde at Snape on 11th June, 1917. The structure located 89 miles 28 chains from Liverpool Street had seven spans ranging from 21 ft 2 in. to 20 ft 3 in., whilst the depth of construction was 3 ft 9 in. In the right background can be seen the arched road bridge spanning the river.

Close up view of timber underbridge No. 1109 spanning the River Alde on the approach to Snape. At high tide the rails were only 5 ft 10 in. above the water level.   *The late B.D.J. Walsh*

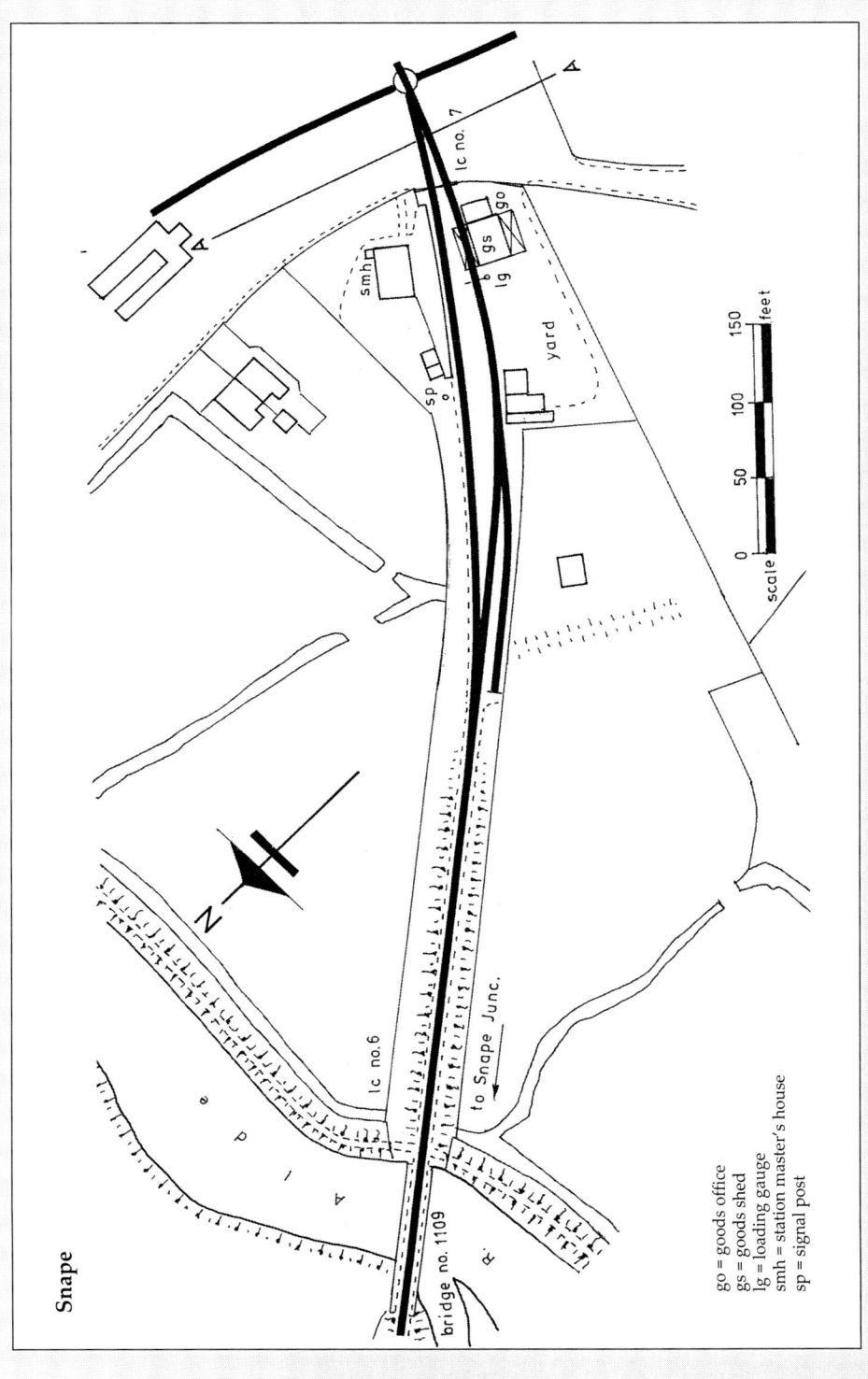

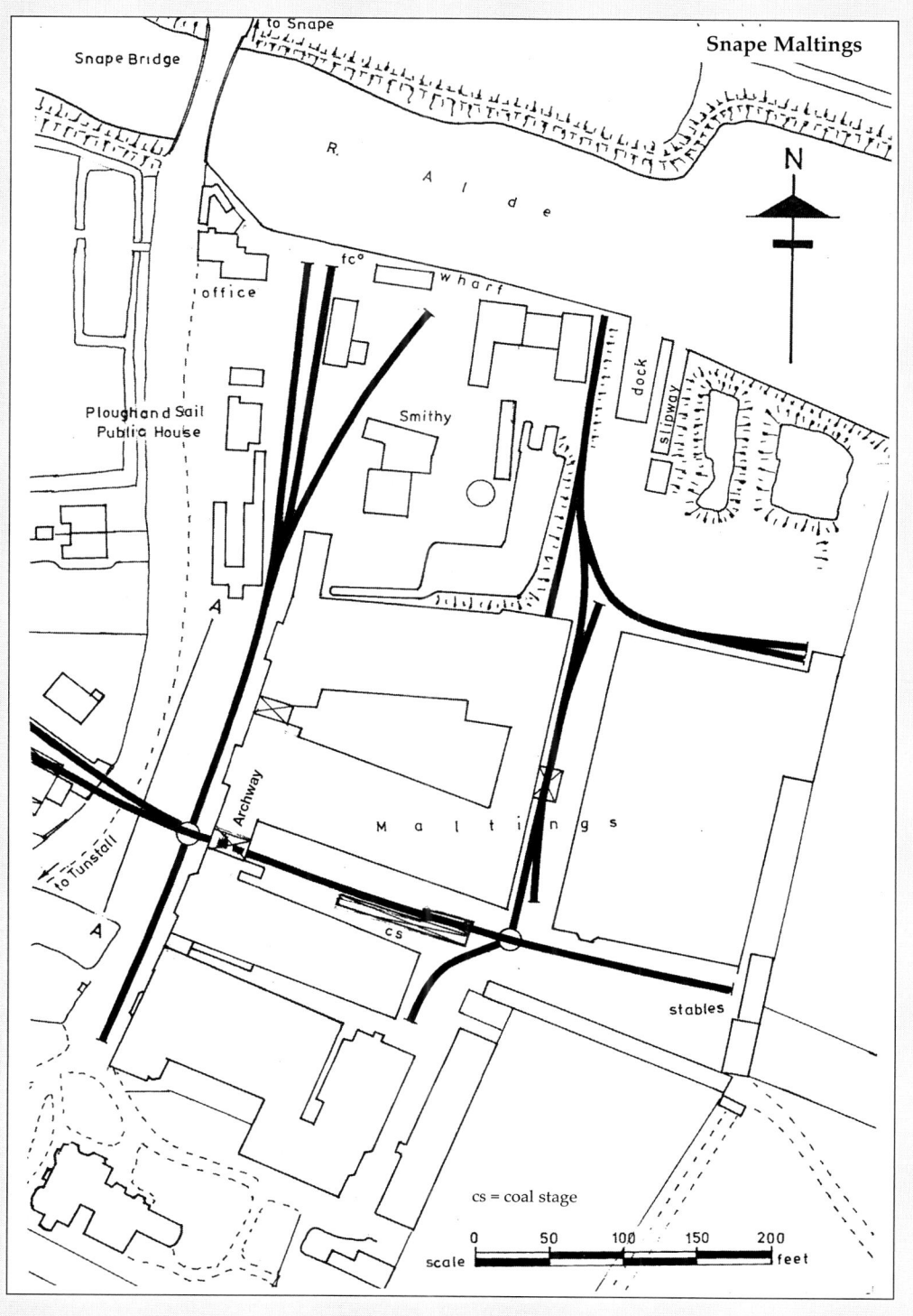

The wide unloading area at Snape and the goods yard throat looking towards Snape Junction with wagons standing on the goods shed road to the left. The bridge over the River Alde was just beyond the points. *The late B.D.J. Walsh*

Having deposited the brake van and an open wagon into the shed loop siding at Snape, 'J15' class No. 65389 has shunted forward and is backing the open wagons into the reception siding. The railway at this point was located on an embankment well above the flood plain of the tidal River Alde. *The late Dr I.C. Allen*

the Concert Hall, whilst the second siding served the repair and shipbuilding dock, and engineers' workshop.

The speed limit of all goods trains throughout the lifespan of the branch line was 15 mph. Railway company locomotives were officially prohibited from crossing the wagon turntable at the entrance to the maltings, and therefore with no run-round facilities available, all trains were supposedly propelled from Snape Junction to Snape and hauled back to the main line. At certain periods when loads were heavy, and to save time, the engine propelled wagons under the arch but with only the tender of the locomotive on the turntable. It was therefore an unwritten rule that all locomotives working the branch operated tender first from Snape Junction to Snape. All shunting beyond railway property and into Snape maltings was performed by horses, although in later years a Fordson petrol-shunting tractor, painted bright blue and orange, was used. At one time a short section of narrow gauge track ran from the malt store to the lower end of Snape Quay. A horse was trained to pull a loaded truck down to the quay and swivel the vehicle round by means of a special collar, which pressed against the side of the truck. This released trip gear, causing the truck to tip up sending the malt down into the hold of the barge. The horse then pulled the empty wagon back to collect another loaded vehicle. By 1958 a short section of the north end or reception loop on railway property was removed as was the siding running along the front of the maltings, thus rendering the turntable in front of the archway redundant, and this was also removed and plain track from the shed road substituted.

Apart from the initial years the normal method of operating the branch involved the weekdays-only pick-up goods train from Ipswich running directly to Saxmundham, where the locomotive ran round its train before working the return service to Ipswich. On arrival at Snape Junction the train reversed and, because of the absence of run round facilities at the terminus, the engine propelled the wagons to Snape with the brake van leading, 10 wagons being the load limit of any propelling movement. If there were more wagons than permitted, the excess vehicles were left in the up reception siding at Snape Junction and the engine returned for them after making the first trip to Snape. After the necessary shunting duties at the goods station, the locomotive hauled the train back to the junction and continued its journey back to Ipswich calling at various intermediate sidings if required. When an engine of unsuitable route availability (i.e. too heavy for the branch) was working the diagram, on returning from Saxmundham any wagons for Snape were left in the up reception siding at Snape Junction, and the train continued as booked to Ipswich. Arrangements were then made for the Framlingham branch engine to work the wagons across the branch. After completing its own branch duties the Framlingham engine propelled a brake van from Wickham Market along the main line to Snape Junction, where it used the trailing crossover to cross to the up line. The brake van was then propelled along the up main clear of the points to the up reception siding, before the engine collected the wagons from the siding. These were reversed on to the brake van and the whole train was then drawn clear of the points leading to the branch, before the locomotive propelled the whole formation to Snape. After the necessary shunting was completed the

Snape goods station, 89 miles 40 chains from Liverpool Street and 1 mile 32 chains from Snape Junction, was provided to serve the maltings opened by Newson Garrett, a prominent member of the local Garrett family, who also established engineering works at Leiston on the neighbouring Aldeburgh branch. 'J15' class 0-6-0 No 65478 stands in the shed road whilst a former London, Midland & Scottish Railway brake van is in the loop road. The remains of the goods shed with only the office standing can be seen in the background. The station, which for many years was served by the weekdays only Ipswich to Saxmundham pick-up goods train on its return working, handled considerable tonnages of barley and malt together with coal and coke for the maltings. From the mid-1920s sugar beet was dispatched to the sugar processing factories at Ipswich, Bury St Edmunds and Cantley, and at one time Snape was reputedly exporting a greater tonnage of beet per annum than any other station in East Anglia.

The late Dr I.C. Allen

Snape station with steam brake-only 'J15' class 0-6-0 tender locomotive No. 65430 shunting a train of covered vans into the reception siding. Note the goods shed in the background and the motor lorry with sacks of malt in the yard. The shed road to the right is also occupied by vans.

The late Dr I.C. Allen

THE ROUTE DESCRIBED

'J15' No. 65389 waits departure in the shed loop at Snape with the branch goods formed of five wagons and a brakevan.
Dr J. Westall/A. Vaughan Collection

Snape goods yard in 1957, with 'J15' class 0-6-0 No. 65478 standing on the shed road waiting to shunt wagons towards the archway into the maltings. The locomotive was only permitted to manoeuvre the vehicles as far as the turntable from where a horse and later a tractor took over to pull or push the vehicles into the maltings complex. The station house is to the left and the remains of the goods shed to the right. At one time a short 170 ft-long siding with points facing up trains ran from the shed line. The gated entrance to the goods yard from the road is to the right of the goods shed.
The late Dr I.C. Allen

Snape goods station facing west in 1929 with the goods shed on the left and ornate station master's house to the right. Note the low platform in front of the latter, which was used for loading and unloading but was later removed. The station house was in a similar East Suffolk Railway style to those on the main line and Framlingham and Aldeburgh branches. The two lines in the foreground crossed the Tunstall to Snape road and merged to meet at a 13 ft 6 in.-diameter wagon turntable, located immediately in front of the archway leading to the inner courtyard of the maltings. Note the iron gates, which when closed marked the boundary of railway property. *Stations UK*

Snape station master's house and maltings in 1959. Although the goods shed was demolished in the winter of 1957/58 the goods shed office is still standing.

engine and train returned immediately to Snape Junction and Wickham Market, where the wagons were left for a forwarding service, whilst the Framlingham branch locomotive resumed its normal branch activities. A further variation occurred when the train from Ipswich was not required to run through to Saxmundham. The train was terminated at Snape Junction and reversed over the trailing crossover from the down main to the up main line, before continuing to Snape. This invariably meant the engine was hauling the train to Snape in contravention of the normal method of working the line. Thus on arrival at the terminus, the engine was uncoupled and ran forward into one siding and clear of the points. The points were changed and a tow rope attached between the coupling on the engine and the coupling on the leading wagon; the train was then set in motion and rolled into the other siding with the guard and goods porter pinning down the brakes. The locomotive then continued shunting in the usual way. If the train consisted of only one or two vehicles the train staff used pinch bars and shunting pole to set the wagons in motion. At other times, railway staff arranged to use the horses, and later the tractor, from Snape maltings to move the vehicles.

A Fordson tractor shunts a seven-plank open wagon past the remains of the goods shed office and over the Tunstall to Snape road towards the maltings in 1959, as the flagman protects the movement.

The archway constructed in 1859 to coincide with the opening of the railway. In the foreground the lines from Snape goods yard converge on the 13 ft 6 in.-diameter wagon turntable, located in front of the arch whence sidings ran north and south along the frontage of the maltings. A third line continued through the arch and ran beside a loading dock, with corrugated iron roof, which was used for offloading coal and coke for the maltings.

Chapter Three

Permanent Way, Signalling and Staff

Permanent Way

The original permanent way of the Snape branch was of two types. The first, similar to that used on the ESR main line, was formed of double-headed rails weighing 68 lb. per yard, fished at the joints with wrought-iron fish plates and screw bolts, secured in cast-iron chairs by ordinary wooden keys. The chairs were fixed to creosoted sleepers by wooden trenails, the sleepers being spaced on average 3 feet apart. The remainder of the track was formed of bridge rails, weighing 60 lb. per yard and fastened by dog spikes to sleepers laid on average 2 feet 4 inches apart. The ballast was formed of gravel and sand. Captain H.W. Tyler, on inspecting the line, stated he would have preferred to see a proportion of iron bolts employed to attach the bridge rails to the sleepers and iron spikes instead of wooden trenails on the curves, where the latter was employed to secure the chairs to the sleepers. The company Engineer advised the inspector that care had been taken to select chairs cast without sharp edges on the lower part of the trenails, in order to safeguard against a shearing action that would otherwise occur on the curves. Tyler pointed out that it was still important to keep a careful watch and that iron spikes be inserted as and when the trenails aged or showed symptoms of failure. The sharpest curve on the branch was noted as 16 chains radius.

In the 1880s some 70 lb. per yard rail in 30 feet lengths replaced the earlier track and by the turn of the century, sections of these were replaced by second-hand bullhead, steel rail weighing 80 lb. per yard (originally weighing 85 lb. per yard). These rails, also in 30 feet lengths, were laid in cast-iron chairs weighing 43 lb. each, secured to the sleepers by two oak trenails and two wrought-iron spikes. The fishplates joining the rails weighed 28 lb. per pair, and were secured by 4⅞ inch steel bolts. The sleepers at this time were of creosoted timber and measured 8 feet 6 inches by 10 inches by 6 inches. Track drainage was carried out by a side ditch and drain pipes.

Soon after Grouping the LNER carried out some remedial replacement of the existing permanent way, especially near Snape Junction, with 85 lb. and 90 lb. per yard bullhead rails, again in 30 feet lengths, but before the outbreak of World War II some 45 feet lengths of rail had been added to the formation. Some of the 30 feet lengths of rail, mounted on chairs bearing the date 1879 and 1880, were still in use on the branch when the line closed in 1960.

The original ballast of gravel and sand was soon found to be inadequate and was replaced by clinker and ashes, which was readily available from the various locomotive depots on ECR/GER/LNER system, notably Ipswich, Lowestoft and Yarmouth South Town. When supplies were unavailable, wagons loads were procured after the mid-1920s from the British Sugar Corporation factories at Ipswich, Cantley and Bury St Edmunds.

The maintenance of the branch came under the jurisdiction of the district engineer of the GER Eastern Division at Ipswich; H. Jones was in office in 1897

Snape Junction and signal box view facing north towards Saxmundham on 30th September, 1956. The signal box, of brick and timber construction, contained a 22 lever McKenzie & Holland frame for working the signals and points on the main line and Snape branch.
The late B.D.J. Walsh

Snape Junction and signal box with the up branch home signal in the foreground. Originally there were signals at Snape as well as the junction but these were removed in 1908, leaving the up distant and up home signals at Snape Junction as the only signalling on the branch. A 'B1' class 4-6-0 tender locomotive passes on the down main line with an express for Lowestoft and Yarmouth South Town in September 1956.
The late B.D.J. Walsh

and for day-to-day affairs the line was controlled by the inspector of No. 6 District also based at Ipswich, T. Baylis in 1897. In 1913 Henry Saunders was ganger covering Snape Junction and the branch. He resided in the cottage at Snape Junction paying an annual rent of £4 11s. 0d. He was still in residence in 1924 by which time the rent had increased to £6 5s. 8d. During this period John Welton was platelayer and lived in Snape Junction crossing cottage rent free, in return for he and his wife opening and closing the gates across the main line, as and when required, for road traffic.

Signalling

The branch was originally worked on the One Engine in Steam principle with a Train Staff but from 1st July, 1873 the Train Staff and Train Staff Ticket method of working was introduced, as laid down in Special Order No. 1550 of the same date. No engine or train was to run on the branch without the Train Staff or Train Staff Ticket. The Train Staff was square in shape, coloured green and lettered 'Snape and Snape Junction'. The paper Ticket was the same colour as the Train Staff. The Train Staff stations were Snape Junction and Snape. From January 1892 the luxury of Ticket working was dispensed with, and the branch was again worked under the One Engine in Steam or two or more coupled together method of working using the Train Staff. The signalman at Snape Junction was the custodian of the Train Staff when not in use. No shunting was to be performed on the main single line at Snape unless the Train Staff was at the station.

From the opening of the line in 1859 a signal hut was located at the junction of the branch with the main line. The signalman had control of certain of the points and the stop signals. Curiously the auxiliary or distant signals were under the control of the crossing keeper at the adjacent Farnham level crossing. Captain Tyler was highly critical of the peculiar arrangement, especially on learning there was no means of communication between the signalman and crossing keeper except by hand signal. As part of the improvements to the East Suffolk main line, an improved signal box was later installed at Snape Junction in 1873, on the up side of the main line, located by the junction points. Further improvements required by the Regulation of Railways Act 1889 were made in 1892, when movements on the main line and to and from the branch were controlled from the new brick and timber signal box containing a 22 lever McKenzie & Holland frame with 5 inch pitch and soldier locking. Distant, home and starting signals were provided in both directions on the main line, whilst distant and home signals protected the junction in the up direction on the branch. There were no branch signals in the down direction. The signal box located on the up side of the main line at 88 miles 08 chains from Liverpool Street was provided with a switching-out lever for the main line only, to permit block signalling between Saxmundham and Wickham Market Junction signal boxes when the box was not in use.

Initially a small hut was provide at Snape to control the signals and points but at the same time as improvements were made at the junction a small signal box was built to control the points and signals at the goods station. Two signals were

Left: Opening and closing times of signal boxes 1910.

Below: Extract from the LNER Working Timetable 1924.

STATIONS AND SIGNAL BOXES.

OPENING AND CLOSING.

Stations.	Signal Boxes.	Distance from Signal Box next above.		REFUGE SIDINGS.		
		Miles.	Chains.	Down.	Up.	
Saxmundham	Snape Junction	...	...	27	27	See East Suffolk Line.
Snape	Station	1	32	...	...	Open on Week-days only from about 1.0 p.m. to 2.30 p.m.

STAFF ONLY

SNAPE JUNCTION TO SNAPE.

SNAPE BRANCH. (Single Line—1 mile 32 chains.)

On Week Days a goods train leaves Snape Junction for Snape at 3.0 p.m. and Snape for Snape Junction at 3.40 p.m.

Only one engine in steam (or two or more engines coupled together) must be allowed on this single line at one and the same time. No engine or train is to be run on this branch without a train staff, no tickets being used. The Train Staff Stations are Snape Junction and Snape. For regulations for working, see Appendix to this Working Time Book.

Saxmundham	Snape Junction	●━━━●	Staff only.	...	...	...
Snape	Station			1	32

SNAPE JUNCTION TO SNAPE.

From 1.10 p.m. until 5.15 p.m. For running of goods trains to and from Snape as required.

		27	27	Ties	Switch provided for Main Line only.

SNAPE BRANCH.

SINGLE LINE. (Distance 1 mile 32 chains.)

Only one engine (or two or more engines coupled together) must be allowed on this single line at one and the same time. No engine or train is to be run on this branch without a TRAIN STAFF, no tickets being used. The Train Staff Stations are Snape Junction and Snape. For regulations for working, see "Appendix."

On Week Days a goods train will run from Snape Junction to Snape and Snape for Snape Junction worked by engine and men of 12.40 p.m. ex Ipswich.

Above: Opening and closing times of signal boxes 1928.

Right: Extract from LNER Working Timetable 1944.

initially provided in the down direction at Snape station, the auxiliary later being replaced by a distant signal located on the approach to the bridge over the River Alde, whilst a stop arm located on a post near the station house protected the road crossing in the down direction. Mounted on the same post was another stop arm, which acted as a starting signal for up trains. These signals were removed early in 1908. The GER had advised the BOT on 23rd December of the previous year that the branch had originally been passed for passenger train working, when inspected in 1859, but as the line was only used for goods traffic, signals would only be provided at Snape Junction. After viewing drawings of the signalling and interlocking at the junction Colonel P.G. Von Donop approved of the arrangements and considered no inspection was necessary. The GER was duly advised on 22nd January, 1908.

The original signalling equipment on the branch, and indeed the main line, was of coloured aspect glasses rotating by action of a connecting rod attached to bell crank levers. The associated semaphore signals were some 15 to 20 feet in height with the arms conveying danger at an angle of 90 degrees to the post, caution at 45 degrees and clear when slotted in the post. During the hours of darkness the revolving spectacles displayed red for danger, green for caution and white for line clear. The auxiliary signals were usually erected some 800 yards in the rear of the semaphore posts, and were kept at 'all right' or clear position except when required to protect a train standing between it and the semaphore signal. This initial signalling was replaced in the late 1870s by the conventional lower quadrant home and distant signals with pitch pine posts, cedar arms and cast- and wrought-iron fittings. In common with GER practice each signal arm was stamped on the reverse with the name of the controlling signal box. Around the turn of the century modifications were made to the operating distant signals at Snape Junction. At that time the GER distant signal arms were painted the same red as stop signals and showed the same red and green aspects to drivers at night. To avoid confusion with the home and starting signals, the distant arms were fitted with Coligny Welch lamps, which displayed an additional white V at night that was actually horizontal (thus >) beside the signal lamp. Because of the low speed and minimal train service, the distant signals on the Snape branch were not modified. With the advent of the LNER all distant signal arms were painted the familiar yellow with black > and the Coligny Welch lamps removed or modified to serve as ordinary lamps on the main line signals. In the latter years the wooden post of the up branch home at Snape Junction was found to be rotting and was replaced by a tubular post with metal upper quadrant arm. Similar changes were made to the signals controlled by Snape Junction signal box on the main line.

On 30th December, 1884, the GER General Manager reported that the East Suffolk line was open for traffic all night but because the speaking telegraphs were in most instances located in station booking offices, which were closed for 11 hours a day, delays occurred to fish and goods trains during these periods. He recommended the provision of a separate signal box circuit between Ipswich and Beccles, including the establishment at Snape Junction, at an estimated cost of £350. The expenditure was duly authorised by the Way and Works Committee. A telegraph connection was also installed between Snape Junction and Snape at the same time. After the abolition of the small signal box at Snape the General Post Office telephone line replaced the railway circuit phone between Snape Junction signal box and Snape station house.

By 1897 Snape Junction signal box was closed and switched out except between the hours of 1.00 pm and 2.45 pm on weekdays only, when it was switched in to allow the passage of the 11.30 am Ipswich to Snape goods to work across the branch. The box was again switched out after the 2.05 pm Snape to Saxmundham goods train had cleared the branch. Snape station signal box was open on weekdays from about 1.00 pm until 2.30 pm. The following year Snape Junction signal box was open on weekdays from 11.30 am until 4.00 pm. The 1906 Appendix to the Working Timetable showed the Junction signal box closed and switched out from 4.00 pm until 12.00 noon on weekdays and from 4.00 pm on Saturdays until 12.00 noon on Mondays from 1st November until 31st May. From 1st June until 31st October the box was closed and switched out from 6.00 pm until 7.00 am on weekdays and from 6.00 pm on Saturdays until 7.00 am on Mondays. Snape signal box was open on weekdays only from about 1.00 pm until 2.30 pm. By 1910 Snape signal box was only open between the hours of 1.00 pm until 2.30 pm weekdays, and in 1919 both Snape Junction and Snape signal boxes were only open from 1.00 pm to 3.30 pm on weekdays.

In 1924 Snape Junction and Snape signal boxes were open between 12.45 pm and 4.05 pm to cater for the running of the branch freight but two years later they were only open for the running of goods trains to and from Snape as required. By 1928 the times had altered to 1.10 pm until 8.15 pm for the Junction signal box, whilst Snape was only open as required for the running of goods trains to and from Snape. In 1937 Snape Junction signal box was open between 1.15 pm to 8.30 pm on weekdays only, whilst Snape signal box was open only for goods trains to and from Snape Junction. Two years later Snape Junction was opened from 1.00 pm to 9.00 pm Mondays to Fridays and 10.00 am to 9.00 pm on Saturdays. Snape signal box was only open for the goods train to and from Snape Junction. These timings continued until 1943, when Snape signal box was abolished and replaced by a ground frame but by 1946 the points were hand operated. In 1947 Snape Junction signal box was opened from 8.00 am to 4.00 pm weekdays only. The same opening times remained until 1950 but by 1952 the opening times were 8.30 am on Fridays and Saturdays or 9.30 am Mondays to Thursdays until 'Train Out of Section' was received for the return Snape goods train. Snape Junction signal box was abolished on 4th December, 1960.

Traffic Staff

From the outset Snape was considered important enough to have the services of a station master. In the 1870s George Maskell, a clerk at Leiston, was appointed station master at Snape Bridge before being promoted to Cockfield on the Bury St Edmunds to Long Melford line and later Darsham. He retired from the GER in 1917 as station master at Walton-on-Naze and died in July 1931. By 1888 he was replaced by William Everitt who remained at Snape until

1907. W.S. (George) Parsons was appointed station master at Snape in July 1907. He entered the service of the GER in August 1885 and ultimately served at the Suffolk goods station until January 1910, when he was promoted to the position of station master at Cold Norton on the Woodham Ferrers to Maldon West branch. Parsons was succeeded by James Crosby, who served at the goods station until after World War I. At the end of 1921 V.E. Collarbone, station master at Barnham on the Bury St Edmunds to Thetford branch, was transferred to take charge at Snape. His stay was short, however, for in December 1922 he was promoted as station master at Cockfield, including Welnetham. The new incumbent was Henry Waller, a clerk in the goods office at Hadleigh who gained promotion to station master at Snape. He remained until January 1927, when he was transferred on promotion to take charge at Felsted, including Rayne, on the Bishop's Stortford to Braintree branch. The position of station master at Snape was of junior grade and was usually the stepping-stone for appointees transferring from clerical positions. The next incumbent was one such individual, George Edward Potter who was promoted from a clerical position at Watton in April 1927. Potter subsequently transferred to Narborough and Pentney, on the Kings Lynn to Dereham line in August 1929 and was succeeded by E. Lee, who was a clerk at Kelvedon, before taking charge at Snape the following month. Two years were enough experience for Lee in a supervisory position and in August 1931 he was appointed as a relief clerk in the District Superintendent's Office at Norwich. In the cutbacks of the 1930s the post of station master was withdrawn and replaced by porter-in-charge and later foreman-in-charge. One of the first incumbents, porter T. Snell died on 10th December, 1938. A goods porter assisted the station master at Snape in the early years but that post was withdrawn in the early 1900s.

With only one train per day serving Snape, the occupant in charge at the goods station could find the job quite monotonous, especially if traffic was minimal. Once wagons were loaded or sheeted or shunted into the maltings or prepared for the outward journey, and consignment notes and wagon labels completed, there was often very little to do, and in summer an occasional swim was taken in the River Alde or a few pints were supped with the locals in the Plough and Sail Public House. At one time a spare set of fishing rods was kept on hand so that the odd hour or two could be whiled away on the riverbank. The difficulty was later compounded by the absence of railway telephonic communication between Snape Junction and Snape. The GPO phone was then located in the station house, which if unattended rang without being answered. Thus when the branch working was made on a bonus trip, the train could enter the branch at any time and on more than one occasion the partly clad foreman-in-charge had to beat a hasty retreat from the river as the train trundled unannounced over the bridge and into Snape station. To obviate delay and save embarrassment the locomotive crews working the branch freight used the engine whistle quite frequently on the approach to the station, so that the staff could be on hand to deal with the traffic as quickly as possible.

Bradshaw's Passenger Timetable for 1862 showing the entry for Snape Junction located 87½ miles from London. There was no equivalent entry in the up direction. The station was never opened.

Chapter Four

Timetables and Traffic

The population of Snape remained almost constant during the years the branch was open, whilst the numbers in the parish of Tunstall, in which the maltings were actually located, steadily declined and it was therefore of no surprise that a passenger service for such small communities, either at Snape or to a station on the main line at Snape Junction, never materialised. Despite various requests and a blank entry against a station in the ESR and *Bradshaw's* timetables between 1859 and 1863, the census figures for Snape and Tunstall confirmed the decision of the ECR officials to refuse the luxury of a passenger service, and the line was thus confined to goods traffic only.

Year	1851	1861	1871	1881	1891	1901	1911	1921	1931	1951	1961
Snape	576	554	546	508	546	529	576	550	603	557	572
Tunstall	676	701	708	615	638	632	591	513	526	489	466

Throughout the life of the line, trains served the Snape branch on weekdays only. Initially the branch was worked by one of the three freight trains running between Ipswich and Yarmouth and return, but from 2nd September, 1859 the number of goods trains was reduced to two in each direction. The resultant reduction meant it was no longer economical for one of these trains to work the branch, and it was agreed the Framlingham branch engine would work the services to and from Wickham Market station goods yard, where wagons could be transferred to and from the Yarmouth to Ipswich goods trains.

Matters soon improved and the GER Working Timetable (WTT) for 1862 showed two goods train in each direction serving the branch. The 10.40 am from Snape Junction and 11.00 am return from Snape ran each weekday, whilst the 4.30 pm from Snape Junction and 4.50 pm from Snape ran on Mondays, Wednesdays and Fridays only. Five minutes running time was permitted for the 1 mile 32 chain journey. The timetable continued in 1863 until 1st June after which the 4.30 pm from Snape Junction and the 4.50 pm return working ran each weekday. By 1865 the services departed Snape Junction at 10.30 am and 4.30 pm, returning from Snape at 10.50 am and 4.50 pm.

The timetable from October 1866 showed the following services on the branch.

Down			a	b	Up			a	b
			am	pm				am	pm
Snape Junction		dep.	10.30	4.30	Snape		dep.	10.50	4.50
Snape		arr.	10.35	4.35	Snape Junction		arr.	10.55	4.55

a Worked by the engine of the 7.20 am goods train from Norwich.
b Worked by the engine of the 2.52 pm goods train from Ipswich.

Snape Branch.—(Single Line.)

Down.		Week Days.							Sundays.		Up.		Week Days.							Sundays.	
Miles from Snape Jn.	FROM	1 Gds.	2 Gds.	3	4	5	6	7	8	9	10	Miles from Snape.	FROM	1 Gds.	2 Gds.	3	4	5	6	7	8	9	10
		a.m.	p.m.											a.m.	p.m.								
	Snape Junction	10 30	4 30	...	...	...	...	...	...	...	...		Snape	10 50	4 50	...	...	...	...	...	...	...	...
1¼	Snape	10 35	4 35	...	...	...	...	...	...	...	...	1¼	Snape Junction	10 55	4 55	...	...	...	...	...	...	...	...

The load of Goods Trains on this Branch is restricted to 15 Trucks.

GER Working Timetable 1865.

SNAPE BRANCH.
Single Line.

Down Trains.		Week Days.											Up Trains.		Week Days.										
Miles from Snape Jn.	FROM	1 A Gds.	2	3	4	5	6	7	8	9	10	11	12	Miles from Snape.	FROM	1 A Gds.	2	3	4	5	6	7	8	9	10	11	12
		a.m.														p.m.											
	Snape Junction ...dep.	1 50	...	...	...	...	...	...	...	...	...	...	...		Snape ...dep.	2 6	...	...	...	...	...	...	...	...	...	...	...
1¼	Snape ...arr.	1 55	...	...	...	...	...	...	...	...	...	...	...	1¼	Snape Junction ...arr.	2 10	...	...	...	...	...	...	...	...	...	...	...

A These Trains are worked by the Engine of the 12.15 p.m. Goods Train from Ipswich.

The load of Goods Trains on this Branch is restricted to 15 Trucks.

October 1, 1870.

GER Working Timetable 1870.

The Trains on this Branch are worked under the Train Staff and Train Ticket arrangements, as laid down in Special Order, No. 1550, dated July 1st, 1873. No Engine or Train is to be run on this Branch without a Train Staff or Train Ticket. The Train Staff Stations are Snape Junction and Snape Station.

SNAPE BRANCH.—*Single Line.*—1¼ *Miles long.*

On Week Days a Goods Train—worked by the 10.25 a.m. Goods Train from Ipswich—leaves Snape Junction for Snape at 12.0 noon, and Snape for Snape Junction at 12.20 p.m.

GER Working Timetable 1875.

The Trains on this Single Line are worked by Train Staff and Train Staff Ticket, according to the "Train Staff Regulations" contained in the "Appendix" to this Working Time Book. No Engine or Train is to be run on this Branch without a Train Staff or Train Staff Ticket. The Train Staff Stations are Snape Junction and Snape Station.

SNAPE BRANCH.—*Single Line.*—1¼ *Miles long.*

On Week Days a Goods Train—worked by the 11.30 a.m. Goods Train from Ipswich—leaves Snape Junction for Snape at 1.50 p.m., and Snape for Snape Junction at 2.35 p.m., except on Saturdays, when a Goods Train—worked by 2.40 p.m. Goods Train from Ipswich—will leave Snape Junction for Snape at 4.30 p.m., and Snape for Snape Junction at 5.0 p.m.

GER Working Timetable 1883.

SNAPE BRANCH.—*Single Line.*—1¼ *Miles long.*

Only one Engine in steam, (or two or more Engines coupled together) *must be allowed on this Single Line at one and the same time. No Engine or Train is to be run on this Branch without a Train Staff; no Tickets being used. The Train Staff Stations are Snape Junction and Snape. For Regulations for working, see pages 125 and 126 of the* "Appendix" *to this Working Time Book.*

On Week Days a Goods Train—worked by the 11.30 a.m. Goods Train from Ipswich—leaves Snape Junction for Snape at 1.40 p.m., and Snape for Snape Junction at 2.5 p.m.

GER Working Timetable 1897.

The June 1867 WTT continued to show a service of two trains in each direction but running at different times on Mondays, Wednesdays and Fridays to that shown on Tuesdays, Thursdays and Saturdays.

Down		a	b	c	d
		am	am	pm	pm
Snape Junction	dep.	9.05	10.30	4.30	6.45
Snape	arr.	9.10	10.35	4.35	6.50

Up		a	b	c	d
		am	am	pm	pm
Snape	dep.	9.25	10.50	4.50	7.05
Snape Junction	arr.	9.30	10.55	4.55	7.10

a Runs Mondays, Wednesdays and Fridays only, worked by the engine of 7.30 am goods train from Ipswich.
b Runs Tuesdays, Thursdays and Saturdays only, worked by the engine of the 7.20 am goods train from Norwich.
c Runs Tuesdays, Thursdays and Saturdays only, worked by the engine of the 2.52 pm goods train from Ipswich.
d Runs Mondays, Wednesdays and Fridays only, worked by the engine of the 3.50 pm goods train from Yarmouth.

After this rather confusing variety, the Working Timetable from April 1868 was simplicity itself, with only one train in each direction across the branch, worked by the engine of the 12.15 pm goods train from Ipswich.

Down				Up			
			pm				pm
Snape Junction	dep.		1.55	Snape	dep.		2.15
Snape	arr.		2.00	Snape Junction	arr.		2.20

By October 1870 the engine of the 12.15 pm from Ipswich was still working the branch but the timetable had been slightly adjusted.

Down				Up			
			pm				pm
Snape Junction	dep.		1.50	Snape	dep.		2.05
Snape	arr.		1.55	Snape Junction	arr.		2.10

The 1875 WTT pronounced, 'On Weekdays a goods train, worked by the 10.25 am goods train from Ipswich leaves Snape Junction for Snape at 12.00 noon and Snape for Snape Junction at 12.20 pm'. These timings remained unaltered until 1883, when the 11.30 am from Ipswich, which departed Snape Junction at 1.50 pm and returned from Snape 2.35 pm, worked the branch on Mondays to Fridays. On Saturdays the line was worked by the 2.40 pm from Ipswich, which left Snape Junction for Snape at 4.30 pm and returned from Snape at 5.00 pm. By 1885 these timings were altered, with the 11.30 am from Ipswich leaving Snape Junction for Snape at 1.45 pm and Snape for Snape Junction at 2.15 pm, except on Saturdays, when the 1.35 pm goods train from Ipswich departed Snape Junction for Snape at 4.00 pm and returned from Snape at 4.30 pm.

The June 1890 WTT still showed the line being worked by the 11.30 am from Ipswich but with the timings on the branch altered, leaving Snape Junction for Snape at 1.35 pm and returning from Snape at 2.05 pm. These timings remained in operation through to 1896. In March 1897 the weekdays-only 11.30 am from Ipswich continued to serve the branch, now departing Snape Junction at 1.40 pm and returning from Snape at 2.05 pm but by July the train ran an hour later from Ipswich at 12.30 pm, departing Snape Junction for Snape at 2.20 pm and returning from Snape at 2.50 pm. In 1899 the 11.40 am from Ipswich worked the branch, leaving Snape Junction for Snape at 1.45 pm and Snape for Snape Junction at 2.05 pm. These timings continued until July 1901 when the train reverted to a 12.30 pm departure from Ipswich, 2.20 pm from Snape Junction to Snape and 2.50 pm return from Snape. In October of the same year the timings reverted to 11.40 am from Ipswich and 1.45 pm from Snape Junction with the 2.05 pm return working. From July 1902 the goods train serving the branch departed Ipswich at the earlier time of 11.00 am but with the altered timing across the branch of 2.20 pm from Snape Junction and 2.50 pm back from Snape. These workings remained in operation until October 1905 when the goods train departed Ipswich at 11.35 am, before entering the branch at 1.45 pm and returning from Snape at 2.05 pm. The July 1906 GER Working Timetable showed the branch being served by the 10.55 am from Ipswich, which departed Snape Junction at 2.20 pm and returned from Snape at 2.50 pm. By March 1907 the departure from Ipswich had reverted to 11.35 am with 1.45 pm from Snape Junction and 2.05 pm return, but in subsequent years reverted to the same timings as in 1906. The GER authorities then appeared undecided as when to run the branch train, for in October 1909 the goods again departed Ipswich at 11.35 am, with the 1.45 pm down run and 2.05 pm up departure on the branch.

The GER WTT for 10th July, 1911 stated, 'On Weekdays a goods train - worked by the 10.55 am goods train from Ipswich - leaves Snape Junction for Snape at 2.20 pm and Snape for Snape Junction at 2.50 pm'. From April of the following year the goods train was again departing Ipswich at 11.35 am, Snape Junction at 1.45pm and returning from Snape at 2.05 pm. From 1st July, 1913 the train reverted to the 10.55 am departure from Ipswich and ran as in the 1911 timetable across the branch, but in the October timetable was put back to 11.35 am with Snape Junction departure time of 1.45 pm and back from Snape at 2.05 pm. From 1st April, 1914 and all through World War I the 10.55 am from Ipswich served the branch, departing Snape Junction for Snape at 2.20 pm and returned from Snape at 2.50 pm. From 1st May, 1918 the train ran slightly earlier across the branch, departing Snape Junction at 1.30 pm and returning from Snape at 2.15 pm. The timetable from 1st March, 1920 showed the same down timing across the branch but the return trip ran 10 minutes later at 2.25 pm.The goods also departed Ipswich at the later time of 11.20 am. From 12th July, 1920 the goods departed Ipswich 10 minutes later at 11.30 am and workings across the branch were adjusted accordingly, with a 1.55 pm departure from Snape Junction and 2.50 pm return from Snape. From 3rd October, 1921 the departure from Ipswich reverted to 11.20 am but timings across the branch were unaltered. The GER Working Timetable from 1st May, 1921 showed later running times across the Snape branch as follows:

Ipswich	*dep.*	11.20 am
Snape Junction	*arr.*	1.50 pm
	dep.	2.20 pm
Snape	*arr.*	2.25 pm
	dep.	3.15 pm
Snape Junction	*arr.*	3.20 pm
	dep.	3.20 pm to Ipswich

Thereafter, for a number of years the WTT omitted any reference to the departure times of the goods train from Ipswich and concentrated on the branch departure times only. From 10th July, 1922 the GER book merely stated, 'On Weekdays a goods train leaves Snape Junction for Snape at 2.25 pm and Snape for Snape Junction at 3.05 pm'. The timings remained in force at Grouping and appeared in the first LNER WTT dating from 9th April, 1923. The new regime then amended the timings from 9th July, 1923, when the train departed Snape Junction at 2.25 pm and returned from Snape at 3.40 pm, only to return to the previous timings from 1st October of the same year. The LNER Working Timetable for 14th July to 21st September, 1924 showed the branch goods departing Snape Junction at 3.00 pm and returning at 3.40 pm, but from 22nd September the train was retimed to depart Snape Junction at 2.25 pm, returning at 3.05 pm. In the summer workings from 13th July to 20th September, 1925, the timings were the same as the previous summer, as were the winter times from 21st September, when the train again departed the junction at 2.25 pm, returning from Snape at 3.05 pm. From 1st December, 1925 the branch train was given a longer standover at Snape with the running times shown as:

		pm
Saxmundham	*dep.*	1.30
Snape Junction	*arr.*	1.35
	dep.	1.45
Snape	*arr.*	1.50
	dep.	3.05
Snape Junction	*arr.*	3.10
	thence to Ipswich	

The LNER WTT from 11th July to 25th September, 1927 showed the weekdays-only goods train leaving Snape Junction at 3.00 pm and back from Snape at 3.40 pm but from 26th September the down train ran at the earlier time of 2.25 pm, returning at 3.05 pm. By 9th July, 1928 the train was departing Snape Junction at the earlier time of 2.15 pm, returning from the terminus at 3.15 pm and these timings continued until 1932. The timetable effective from 1st May, 1933 showed separate timings for the down train on Mondays to Fridays, which departed Snape Junction at 2.35 pm, and Saturdays only when the train departed at 2.50 pm. The up working departed Snape at 3.15 pm each weekday. These timings continued in operation until 9th July, 1934, when the down train departed Snape Junction at 2.35 pm each weekday and returned from Snape at 3.15 pm. The only alteration shown in the timetable effective from 8th July, 1935, was the down train which ran 10 minutes later but from 30th September the goods trains departing Snape Junction at 2.35 pm Saturdays excepted (SX) and 2.50 pm Saturdays only (SO), returned from Snape at the uniform time of 3.15 pm.

From 6th July, 1936 the down working reverted to the 2.45 pm departure from Snape Junction and 3.15 pm return from Snape but from 28th September both trains ran 10 minutes earlier. The subsequent summer timetable effective from 5th July, 1937 reverted to similar timings as July 1936. From 27th September the branch train departed from the junction at 2.35 pm and returned from Snape at 3.05 pm. The following summer timetable operative from 4th July, 1938 showed the SO train running at the latest time in the day since 1867.

		SX	SO
		pm	pm
Snape Junction	dep.	2.45	4.20
Snape	arr.	2.55	4.25
Snape	dep.	3.15	5.10
Snape Junction	arr.	3.20	5.15

The main line Working Timetable from 3rd July, 1939 and subsequent issues, showed no intermediate timings for trains serving the branch, and merely advised an engine and men from Ipswich worked the service. The appointed train called at intermediate stations on the East Suffolk line, if required to shunt the goods yards, and terminated at Saxmundham at some indefinite time before returning to Ipswich via Snape, again without timings being given. These were later to become 'bonus workings' for Ipswich footplatemen, who worked the train out and back as quickly as possible, running to control instructions. Thus from July 1939 the engine and men of the 9.10 am (SO) and 12.45 pm (SX) ex-Ipswich worked the branch goods train but from 2nd October the (SX) working departed at the earlier time of 12.35 pm. These trains continued to run until 7th July, 1941 when the 12.35 pm (SX) Ipswich to Snape and return on Mondays was retimed to start at 9.10 am and ran as on Saturdays. The crew were to ensure the train returned as soon as possible from Snape, before the engine performed shunting and general assistance at Wickham Market in connection with cattle traffic, leaving for Ipswich when ready. The WTT when reissued from 6th October, 1941, advised the goods train would run from Snape Junction to Snape and return worked by the engine and men of the 9.10 am Mondays and Saturdays only and 12.35 pm Mondays and Saturdays excepted ex-Ipswich. From 3rd May, 1943 until 30th April, 1944 the engine and men of the 12.35 pm ex-Ipswich worked the branch but from 1st May, 1944 the train was retimed to start at 12.40 pm. The revised timing remained in operation until 6th May, 1946, when the WTT advised the line would be worked by the engine and men of the 12.25 pm train from Ipswich. From 16th June, 1947, however, the goods train reverted to a 12.40 pm departure from the Suffolk town.

The British Railways administration must have been satisfied with the arrangements for working the Snape branch, for timings remained unaltered until 26th September, 1949, when the train departure time was put back five minutes to 12.45 pm. A year later the timings were again put back to 12.50 pm from Ipswich but from 18th June, 1951 reverted to 12.45 pm departure, before again changing to 12.50 pm from 10th September, 1951. The timetable effective from 30th June, 1952 announced, 'On weekdays a goods train will run from Snape Junction to Snape and back worked by the engine and men of the 12.55

pm ex-Ipswich'. The next timetable operative from 15th September, 1952 was the last to show such an entry, for from 8th June, 1953 the timetable merely showed the return working of the 1.05 pm goods train ex-Ipswich to Saxmundham serving Snape. From 20th September, 1954 the train ran at different times 1.05 pm (SO) and 1.10 pm (SX), only to revert to the standard time of 1.05 pm from Ipswich on and from 13th June, 1955. The winter timetable from 19th September returned to the 1.05 pm (SO) and 1.10 pm (SX) departures from Ipswich to Saxmundham, but from 11th June, 1956 the return working of the 1.03 pm ex-Ipswich to Saxmundham served the Snape branch. In the 1950s lack of traffic often meant the train ran across the branch on Wednesdays only as a 'bonus' working.

The BR (ER) WTT entry from 17th September, 1956 set the precedent for future operation of the branch and showed the 9.50 am SO, 11.12 am (SX), ex-Ipswich goods yard as running to Wickham Market and Framlingham, thence to Wickham Market and Saxmundham, returning to Snape Junction and Snape, and from Snape via Wickham Market and Woodbridge to Ipswich goods yard. No intermediate or arrival times were specified. From 17th June the (SO) working departed at the earlier time of 8.45 am and these timings remained in operation until 5th January, 1959, when the (SX) working was retimed to depart eight minutes later at 11.20 am. The timetable for 15th June to 13th September, 1959, which remained in operation until 1st November continued to show the departures from Ipswich at 8.45 am (SO) and 11.20 am (SX), but from 2nd November until 5th March, 1960 the (SX) working departed at 11.25 am. By this time proposals to withdraw the service were well advanced and the Working Timetable effective from 7th March, 1960, tersely advised that the 8.45 am (SO) and 11.25 am (SX) ex-Ipswich goods yard would not run, 'Snape branch closed to all traffic'.

Goods Traffic

Before the coming of the railway, commodities were brought to the Snape maltings and surrounding hamlets by sailing barge along the River Alde, or by pack horse or horse-drawn waggons along the dusty roads in summer, which quickly turned to quagmires in the rain and snows of winter. The Snape branch was built essentially as a long siding from the East Suffolk main line to serve Newson Garrett's maltings and, once opened, malting barley was the chief import, together with coal and coke used for drying the kilns. Lime and general merchandise was also received for the local farming community. In return sacks of malt were dispatched by rail to breweries in London and East Anglian towns. When the opening of the railway was announced, H. Edwards, a local corn and seed merchant, advertised that he would send his wares by train from Woodbridge to any station including Snape. The rates charged by the ESR were exorbitant and the expected transfer of freight from road and water to rail did not come up to expectations. On 24th September, 1859, the ESR agreed to reduce the conveyance charges for grain, oil cake and manure from Melton and Woodbridge to Snape from 4s. 0d. to 2s. 6d. per ton. Similar reductions were made from Snape

BR (ER) Working Timetable 1955.

to Melton, Wickham Market and Marlesford. By 1874 Thomas William Girling was also established as a corn and coal merchant at Snape and used the railway for receipt and dispatch of goods. Spare equipment for the maintenance and repair of the maltings was also transported by rail, together with smalls traffic for Snape and Tunstall villages. Other imports included spares and equipment for the maintenance and repairs of barges and sailing vessels docking at Snape. Building materials, especially for the extension to the maltings, manufactured goods and agricultural products and machinery also arrived by train. In the late 1920s and early 1930s many of the country roads were still unmetalled and Suffolk County Council undertook a rolling programme of road improvements. This involved levelling the surface before covering with granite chippings and tarmacadam. Much of the material was delivered by rail to Snape, where the material was offloaded and taken to site by horse and waggon. The granite and tarmacadam was then levelled by steamroller.

Over the years the railway and river did not have the complete monopoly of the barley traffic to Snape, for the locally grown commodity continued to be carted in tumbrils and later red and black painted waggons, pulled by pairs of Suffolk Punch horses. The waggoners in billycock hats or caps usually quaffed a pint of mild in the Plough and Sail Inn before returning home. From the 1930s road lorries increasingly replaced the horse and cart.

In the early years of the branch, some fish traffic was landed and forwarded by the daily goods train but the commodity quickly disappeared when the catches were landed at ports offering better rail facilities. Small amounts of livestock were also conveyed to and from the goods terminus over the years, although offloading was difficult in the absence of a cattle loading dock and cattle pens, and when necessary the low platform fronting the station house was used for such purposes. From the late 1920s local farmers cultivated an increasing acreage of sugar beet and during season from October to February, a considerable tonnage was regularly sent from Snape to the sugar processing factories at Ipswich, Bury St Edmunds and Cantley. In the years after World War II the sugar beet conveyance often exceeded the barley and malt tonnages and it was boasted that in some weeks of the campaign more sugar beet was loaded at Snape than at any other station in East Anglia. S. Swonnell & Sons finally ceased sending malt and barley by rail in the early 1950s. The firm, however, continued to receive wagon loads of coal and coke until the closure of the line in March 1960. Coal and coke had also been transported regularly to Snape for domestic purposes, and over the years several fuel traders distributed to Snape, Tunstall, Iken and other small communities in the area.

Parcels traffic was regularly handled at Snape but during the early months of operation the tariff charged by the ESR was excessive and local carriers continued to convey most items. In an effort to attract traffic and compete with the road carriers, the ESR and ECR Joint Committee agreed to a reduction of 6*d*. to 4*d*. a parcel at their meeting on 24th September, 1859. Parcel traffic, however, was never excessive and typical receipts for the years 1923 to 1928 showed fairly constant numbers, but after 1924 takings reduced because of the introduction of cheaper cartage rates.

Having breasted 1 in 66/249 climb off the branch 'J15' class No. 65430 passes Snape Junction up branch home signal and makes for Wickham Market with her train of three covered vans, four open wagons and brake van. The fireman can be seen holding the Snape Junction to Snape single line Train Staff ready to hand it over to the signalman. *The late Dr I.C. Allen*

The branch train being propelled down the branch towards Snape by 'J15' class 0-6-0 No. 65430. The wide formation suggests land was purchased for the building of a double track railway, but only a single track branch was planned and built. *The late Dr I.C. Allen*

'J15' class 0-6-0 No. 65478 shunting an empty open wagon into the up reception siding at Snape Junction on a wintry day. Note the absence of buffer stops, which had been demolished in a rough shunt some years earlier and never replaced. The down reception siding is on the left.
The late Dr I.C. Allen

After depositing the 16 ton all-steel mineral wagon in the up reception siding at Snape Junction, 'J15' class No. 65478 returns to the main line with the van before backing on to her train and continuing the journey to Wickham Market. To the right is the railway cottage originally built to accommodate the signalman and his family at this isolated location. A similar cottage was provided for the crossing keeper at the nearby Farnham/Snape level crossing seen in the background.
The late Dr I.C. Allen

The Suffolk landscape appears cold and bleak as 'J15' class 0-6-0 No. 65478 climbs the bank towards Snape Junction in January 1958.
The late Dr I.C. Allen

A delicate shunting manoeuvre is carried out at Snape Junction on a chilly winter's day. 'J15' class 0-6-0 No. 65478 has detached a covered van and open wagon from the rest of the train standing on the branch. The open wagon had developed a hot axlebox *en route* from Snape and is being shunted into the up reception siding to await attention by the carriage and wagon examiner from Ipswich.
The late Dr I.C. Allen

TIMETABLES AND TRAFFIC

	Parcels	Receipts £
1923	490	71
1924	432	41
1925	449	42
1926	481	39
1927	434	38
1928	451	38

The following goods facilities were available at Snape.

Fixed Crane	1 ton 10 cwt capacity
Truck Weighbridge	20 tons capacity
Weighing Machine	1 ton 12 cwt capacity
Goods Shed	
Loading Gauge	

The station had facilities for lifting vans by crane power and the latest time for acceptance of traffic for forwarding the same day was 1.30 pm. The use of tow ropes for shunting duties was permitted in cases of emergency only, but this rule was often abused in the latter days when the engine arrived at the Snape end of the train.

The load limit on the branch from 1870 was 15 wagons, whilst the maximum number of wagons permitted to be propelled across the branch was 10 vehicles. In later years the GER Appendix to the Working Timetable showed the following permitted loads.

	Goods Trucks Loaded		Coal Trucks Loaded	
	Down	Up	Down	Up
First Class Engines	35	25	30	20
Second Class Engines	30	20	25	15

The loadings were later amended to:

Class of Engine	Mineral		Goods	
	Down	Up	Down	Up
A	40	30	40	40
B	34	20	40	28
C	29	18	40	26
D	26	16	37	23
E	24	14	34	20
F	23	13	33	18
G	20	12	28	17
H	18	11	26	15

Locomotives regularly allocated to the branch workings were,

GER Class	LNER Class	Type	Classified
Y14	J15	0-6-0	C
C32	F3	2-4-2T	E

'J15' class 0-6-0 tender locomotive No. 65459 propelling a wagon and brake van from the down main line to the up main line via the trailing crossover at Snape Junction, prior to taking the train on to the Snape branch. In the background is Farnham/Snape level crossing No. 54 and its associated crossing keeper's cottage. *The late Dr I.C. Allen*

'J15' class 0-6-0 No. 65478 propels her brake van along the down main line away from Wickham Market Junction *en route* for Snape with the 'bonus' goods after working the Framlingham branch, which can be seen diverging behind the train. *The late Dr I.C. Allen*

Snape Junction up reception siding with 'J15' class 0-6-0 No. 65389 depositing an engineers' coach to be used as a mess and tool van for staff working on track maintenance at the junction.
The late Dr I.C. Allen

Ancient and modern; Brush type '2', 1,250 hp diesel electric locomotive No. D5500 passing Snape Junction with the up Halesworth milk train in October 1959 as 'J15' class 0-6-0 No. 65478 waits at the home signal with the Snape branch goods. Note the catch points in the up reception siding and in the Snape branch single line.
The late Dr I.C. Allen

There is no outgoing traffic from Snape as 'J15' class 0-6-0 No. 65478 passes Botany Wood and climbs the 1 in 66 gradient on the approach to Snape Junction with her attendant brake van. Note the short length bullhead track, which survived on the Snape branch until closure in March 1960.
The late Dr I.C. Allen

Snape has provided no outgoing traffic so 'J15' class 0-6-0 No. 65478 and brake van leave the branch at Snape Junction *en route* to Wickham Market in October 1959. To the left the down reception siding can be seen running parallel to the down main line. *The late Dr I.C. Allen*

Snape River underbridge No. 1109 spanning the River Alde was the main engineering structure on the branch and like the two other bridges was constructed of timber. A severe restriction was imposed on the line and only the lightest of locomotives could work the daily goods service. Both the LNER and British Railways classified the line under Route Availability 2 (RA2) with the 'J15' class 0-6-0 tender locomotives being regularly utilised for many years. All too frequently in the latter years there was no outgoing traffic from Snape and here 'J15' No. 65389 returns to Snape Junction with the brake van before continuing to Wickham Market and intermediate stations to Ipswich. *The late Dr I.C. Allen*

'J15' class 0-6-0 No. 65389 and train cross the river bridge into Snape. As there was no traffic for Saxmundham and to save time, the down train from Ipswich had reversed at Snape Junction and run directly on to the branch with the engine at the Snape end of the train. The engine was released by leaving the brake van and wagons on the main single line before running forward into the shed road. The points were then changed and the brake van and wagons hauled into the reception loop by tow-rope attached to the engine. *The late Dr I.C. Allen*

'J15' class 0-6-0 No. 65389 departs from Snape and crosses the river bridge on a cold and raw winter's day with a train formed of an assortment of open wagons. Snape maltings can be seen in the background, partially obscured by smoke. *The late Dr I.C. Allen*

GER engine Nos. 10 to 19, 1150 to 1219 and 1850 to 1900 were prohibited from running across the branch. Later, engines in classes 'A' and 'B' were also banned from the branch.

The LNER freight train loads book showed the following permitted loads:

Wickham Market to Snape	Minerals	Goods	Empties
No. 1 Class	26	39	40
No. 2 Class	29	40	40
No. 3 Class	22	40	40

Snape to Wickham Market	Minerals	Goods	Empties
No. 1 Class	16	24	30
No. 2 Class	17	25	30
No. 3 Class	19	28	30

The length of trains was limited to 40 wagons on the branch. British Railways Eastern Region later amended the loading limits to,

Snape Junction to Snape	Heavies	Goods	Empties
No. 1 Class	23	40	40
No. 2 Class	26	40	40
No. 3 Class	29	40	40

Snape to Snape Junction	Heavies	Goods	Empties
No. 1 Class	14	25	28
No. 2 Class	15	26	30
No. 3 Class	17	30	34

The 'J15' class 0-6-0 tender locomotive was a class '3' engine.

The load limit of 40 wagons was never worked and the limit tended to be kept to 10 vehicles on the down working and the same number on the up although if most were empties this was increased to 15.

Chapter Five

Locomotives and Rolling Stock

From the outset the Snape branch was essentially a goods line and although several requests were made for a passenger service, no such facilities were offered. The permanent way was of light construction and, together with three timber underbridges, meant that only locomotives with low axle loading could work the goods services. The ECR, EUR and ultimately GER fortunately possessed ample engines of low route availability to work the line. In GER days, locomotives working the Snape branch were limited to a weight of 40 tons. The LNER initially only permitted 'E4' class 2-4-0s and 'J15' class 0-6-0 tender locomotives and 'Y1', 'Y3', 'Y5', 'Y6' and 'Y10' 0-4-0 tank locomotives on the line, but it is almost certain none of the latter ever worked across the branch. The LNER and later BR classified the branch to Route Availability 2 (RA2) with no allowance for heavier classes. Because of the weak timber underbridges on the line, double-heading was prohibited. With the lack of locomotive watering facilities, it was an unwritten rule that the line was to be worked by tender locomotives only.

In the mists of time it is uncertain which locomotives worked the Snape branch at the outset or indeed individual engine numbers, but from various sources the following are known to have worked the East Suffolk line freight trains, including the short return workings on the branch. In March and April 1846 Stothert & Slaughter built five 0-6-0 goods tender engines for the ECR. They were originally numbered 97 to 101 but were soon renumbered 155 to 159 and were delivered with six-wheel tenders. In 1858 the tenders received new tanks giving a greater water capacity and although the first two were early casualties for scrapping, Nos. 157 to 159 were placed on the duplicate list in 1864 becoming Nos. 1570, 1580 and 1590 respectively. The first two were rebuilt with new boilers in 1866 and were sent away to Cambridge to work goods trains to Colchester via Sudbury and the Colne Valley & Halstead Railway. No. 1590 was scrapped in April 1873, No. 1580 in August 1880 and 1570 in October 1883. The leading dimensions of the class were:

Cylinders		16 in. x 24 in.
Boiler	Outside diameter	3 ft 9 in.
	Length	10 ft 2 in.
Firebox		4 ft 8 in.
Heating surface	Tubes 152 x 1⅞ in.	
Driving wheels		5 ft 0 in.
Wheelbase	Locomotive	13 ft 8 in.
Water capacity		1,350 gallons
Weight in working order		24 tons 18 cwt*
Max. axle loading		10 tons 3 cwt*

* after rebuilding

Another class used in the early years was R. Stephenson & Company's 'Long Boiler' 2-4-0 tender locomotives, delivered to the ECR between March and September 1847. Numbered in the series 71 to 77 they regularly worked the East

ECR Stothert & Slaughter 0-6-0 tender locomotive No. 155.

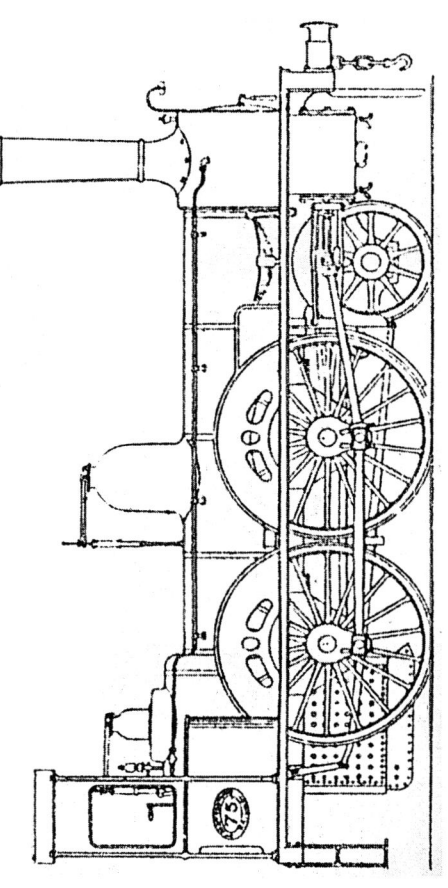

Robert Stephenson & Company 'Long Boiler' 2-4-0 tender locomotive No. 75.

Suffolk line in the first decade after opening. They were the subject of several modifications and rebuildings, Nos. 71 and 77 receiving new boilers in 1860 whilst Nos. 72 and 75 were rebuilt in June 1867. Several were placed on the duplicate list, Nos. 71, 72 and 75 becoming 710, 720 and 750 respectively in 1876. The locomotives were scrapped as follows, No. 710 in May 1878, 720 in September 1877, 73 in November 1869, 74 in April 1859, 750 in April 1881, 76 in July 1868 and 77 in August 1871. The principal dimensions of the class as modified by Robert Sinclair, the locomotive superintendent of the ECR and GER from 1856 to 1866, were:

Cylinders		15 in. x 22 in.
Boiler	Max. diameter	3 ft 8 in.
	Length	13 ft 8½ in.
Firebox		4 ft 2 in.
Heating surface	Tubes 123 x 1⅞ in.	838.5 sq. ft
	Firebox	67.6 sq. ft
	Total	906.1 sq. ft
Grate area		10.8 sq. ft
Boiler pressure		110 psi
Leading wheels		3 ft 6 in.
Coupled wheels		6 ft 0 in.
Wheelbase		11 ft 7 in.

Between 1854 and 1855 John V. Gooch, locomotive superintendent of the ECR from 1850 to 1856, introduced into service five six-coupled goods engines with fairly new boilers taken from five large Crampton singles which were scrapped through lack of adhesion. The five numbered 233 to 237 were built at Stratford works and had outside bearings. They served at Ipswich for a while and worked the East Suffolk freight services. New boilers designed by Sinclair were fitted to Nos. 234 and 236 in October 1867, whilst Johnson rebuilt the remaining three in 1869 and 1870. The five engines were placed on the duplicate list in 1880 by having a cipher added to their running number but only survived for a few more years in service, No. 234 being scrapped in April 1882, Nos. 233 and 235 in January 1883, No. 237 in October 1883 and 236 in November 1884. The leading dimensions of the Samuel W. Johnson* rebuilt engines were

Cylinders		16 in. x 24 in.
Boiler	Max. outside diameter	4 ft 0 in.
	Length	9 ft 11¼ in.
Firebox		5 ft 1¾ in.
Grate area		15.5 sq. ft
Heating surface	Tubes 157 x 2 in.	841.5 sq. ft
	Firebox	89.65 sq. ft
	Total	931.15 sq. ft
Boiler pressure		140 psi
Driving wheels		5 ft 0 in.
Wheelbase	Engine	14 ft 6 in.
	Tender	10 ft 2 in.
Weight in working order	Engine	27 tons 7 cwt
	Tender	17 tons 1 cwt
	Total	44 tons 8 cwt
Max. axle loading		10 tons 15 cwt

* GER locomotive superintendent from 1866 -1873.

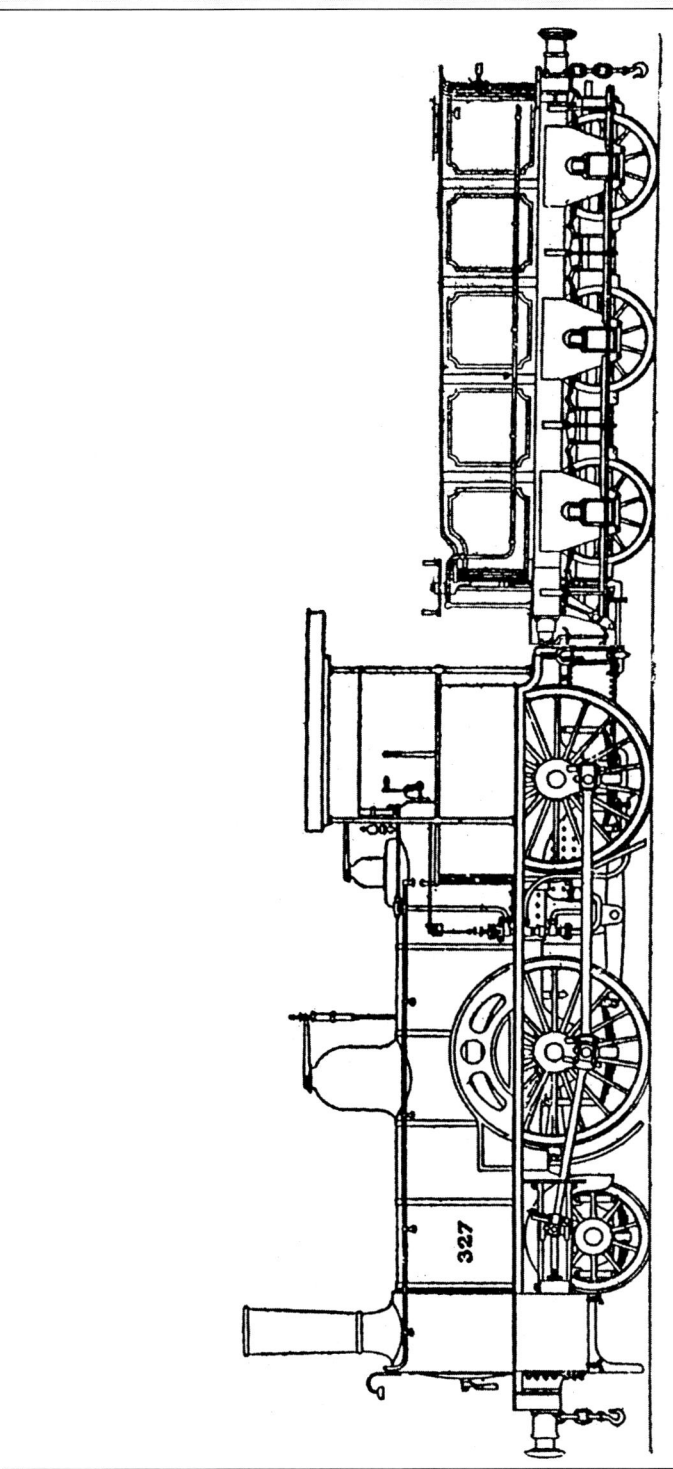

Sinclair 'Y' class 2-4-0 tender locomotive.

LOCOMOTIVES AND ROLLING STOCK

The next locomotives to work the Snape services were Sinclair's celebrated 'Y' class 2-4-0 goods engines. Between July 1859 and August 1866 one hundred and ten were introduced into service from a variety of makers, Neilson and Company building Nos. 307 to 326, Robert Stephenson and Company Nos. 327 to 341, R. & W. Hawthorn Nos. 342 to 356, Kitson and Company Nos. 357 to 381, Vulcan Foundry Nos. 382 to 406 and Schnider et Cie of Creusot Nos. 407 to 416. Each batch had detailed differences and engine No. 327 was displayed at the Exhibition held in Hyde Park, London in 1862. The engines worked all over the GER system on passenger, goods and mixed traffic services and those allocated to Ipswich spent considerable time on express and trip goods diagrams. Over the years most were rebuilt and a number were converted into 4-4-0 tender locomotives for passenger work. Scrapping of the class commenced in 1882 and after 1888 surviving engines were placed on the duplicate list by having a prefix '0' placed before the running number. The class only saw service on the Snape branch in their declining years. The final batch of four locomotives was condemned in 1894.

The leading dimensions of the 327 to 356 batch of locomotives as built were:

Cylinders		17 in. x 24 in.
Boiler	Max. outside diameter	4 ft 0 in.
	Length	11 ft 5¾ in.
Firebox		4 ft 8 in.
Heating surface	Tubes 192 x 1⅞ in.	968.52 sq. ft
	Firebox	72.36 sq. ft
	Total	1040.88 sq. ft
Grate area		13.75 sq. ft
Boiler pressure		120 psi
Leading wheels		3 ft 7 in.
Coupled wheels		6 ft 1 in.
Tender wheels		3 ft 7 in.
Wheelbase	Engine	15 ft 1 in.
	Tender	11 ft 5 in.
Weight in working order	Engine	30 tons 16 cwt
	Tender	21 tons 15 cwt
	Total	52 tons 11 cwt
Water capacity		1,600 gallons

From the 1880s Samuel Johnson's '417' class 0-6-0 tender locomotives worked the branch services. They were originally introduced between 1867 and 1869 and built by Neilson & Company and the Worcester Engine Company. The 60 built were numbered 417 to 476 and initially worked main line goods trains but on the introduction of the '477' class and 'Y14' class 0-6-0 tender locomotives were relegated to pick-up freights and branch line work. The various members of the class allocated to Ipswich depot worked out their last years on the East Suffolk line, which included the trip to Snape. The first of the class was withdrawn in 1888 and scrapping continued every year, with the exception of 1897, until 1899. The survivors after 1891 were placed on the duplicate list by having an '0' prefix added to the number. The leading dimensions of the class were:

Sinclair 'Y' class 2-4-0 goods engine used on Snape branch services in their declining years when they were placed on the duplicate list by having a prefix '0' placed before the running number. No. 0396 at Norwich is typical of the class
LCGB/Ken Nunn

ECR Gooch 0-6-0 tender locomotive No. 235 as rebuilt by Johnson.

Cylinders	2 inside	16½ in. x 24 in.
Motion		Stephenson with slide valves
Boiler	Max. dia. outside	4 ft 2 in.
	Length	10 ft 0 in.
Firebox		5 ft 5 in.
Heating surface	Tubes 203 x 1¾ in.	957.6 sq. ft
	Firebox	94.9 sq. ft
	Total	1052.5 sq. ft
Grate area		15.27 sq. ft
Boiler pressure		140 psi
Driving wheels		5 ft 3 in.
Tender wheels		3 ft 7 in.
Wheelbase	Engine	15 ft 3 in.
	Tender	9 ft 0 in.
Weight in working order	Engine	30 tons 15 cwt
	Tender	21 tons 17 cwt
	Total	52 tons 12 cwt
Max. axle loading		11 tons 5 cwt
Water capacity		1,740 gallons

The next class to be associated with the Snape branch goods services was the '477' series 0-6-0 tender locomotives, designed by Samuel Johnson and dating from 1871 to 1873. Numbered in the series 477 to 526, the class came from a variety of builders, Beyer, Peacock, Robert Stephenson, Dübs, Nasmyth Wilson and the Yorkshire Engine Company. All were rebuilt between 1888 and 1895. By the time they were used on the Snape branch goods, the engines had relinquished their main line goods turns and were relegated to branch line and secondary duties. Nos. 477 to 496 were placed on the duplicate list by having a prefix '0' added to the running number in 1894, whilst Nos. 497 to 506 were similarly treated in 1896. The remaining locomotives still in service were added to the duplicate list in 1899, and these survivors were withdrawn between 1897 and 1902. The principal dimensions of the class were:

Cylinders	2 inside	17 in. x 24 in.
Motion		Stephenson with slide valves
Boiler	Max. dia. outside	4 ft 2 in.
	Barrel length	10 ft 0 in.
	Firebox outside length	5 ft 5 in.
Heating surface	Tubes 223 x 1⅝ in.	980.0 sq. ft
	Firebox	94.9 sq. ft
	Total	1074.9 sq. ft
Grate area		15.27 sq. ft
Boiler pressure		140 psi
Coupled wheels		5 ft 2 in.
Tender wheels		3 ft 8 in.
Wheelbase	Engine	15 ft 6 in.
	Tender	12 ft 0 in.
Weight in working order	Engine	32 tons 13 cwt
	Tender	26 tons 5 cwt
	Total	58 tons 18 cwt
Max. axle loading		12 tons 6 cwt
Water capacity		2,038 gallons

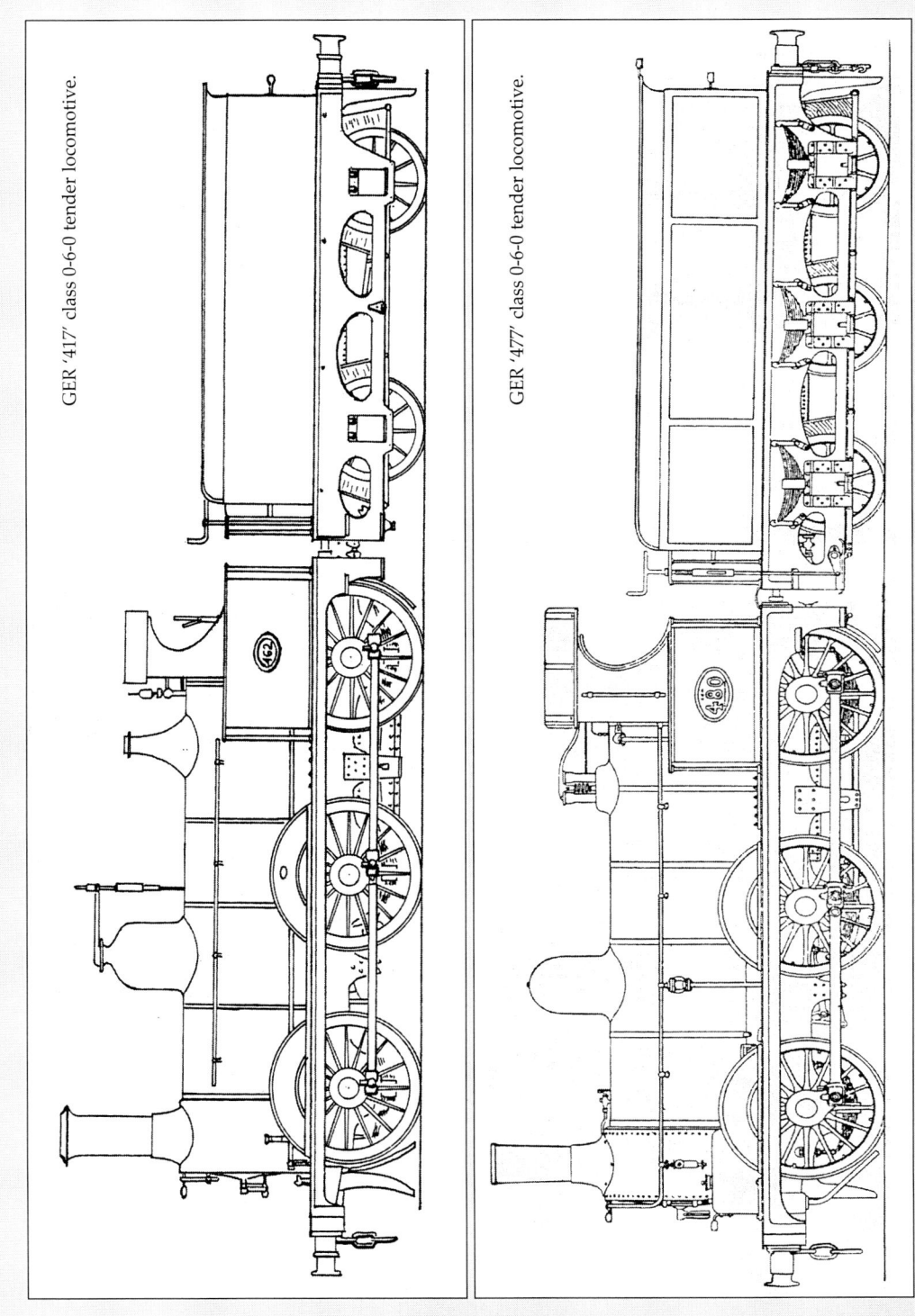

LOCOMOTIVES AND ROLLING STOCK

After the withdrawal of the '477' class, the freight traffic was placed in the hands of the GER 'Y14' class 0-6-0 tender locomotives designed by T.W. Worsdell. Introduced in 1883, these small engines were later classified 'J15' by the LNER. Such was the success of the design that building continued until 1913. All except 19 of the class of 289 were built at Stratford works, the others being constructed by Sharp, Stewart & Company. Because of the low RA1 route availability this ubiquitous class was ideal for working the Snape branch and they continued to do so for over 60 years until the withdrawal of services in March 1960. Locomotives known to have worked the branch included:

GER No.	LNER 1924 No.	LNER 1946 No.	BR No.	Condemned
37	7037	–	–	August 1923
38	07038	–	–	September 1932
39	07039	–	–	March 1933
40	–	–	–	October 1922
509	7509	5429	–	November 1950
510	7510	5430	65430	January 1956
525	7525	–	–	October 1935
537	–	–	–	August 1923
538	7538	–	–	December 1938
542	7542	5470	65470	December 1959
545	7545	5473	65473	March 1960
546	7546	5474	65474	February 1960
550	7550	5478	65478	October 1961
556	7556	5454	65454	May 1959
559	7559	5457	65457	February 1962
561	7561	5459	65459	February 1960
566	7566	5464	65464	September 1962
568	7568	5466	65466	July 1958
569	7569	5467	65467	February 1959
570	7570	5468	65468	September 1959
592	7592	–	–	August 1928
593	7593	–	–	December 1926
594	7594	–	–	July 1926
595	7595	–	–	June 1929
596	7596	–	–	November 1932
597	7597	–	–	April 1928
598	7598	–	–	September 1926
599	7599	–	–	May 1931
641	7641	5441	65441	October 1958
642	7642	5442	65442	May 1958
647	7647	5447	65447	April 1959
693	7693	–	–	July 1928
694	7694	–	–	October 1931
836	7836	5361	65361	September 1962
866	7866	5377	–	February 1951
875	7875	5382	–	March 1952
883	7883	5388	65388	May 1959
886	7886	5389	65389	April 1960
897	7897	5396	–	March 1951
910	7910	5404	65404	October 1956

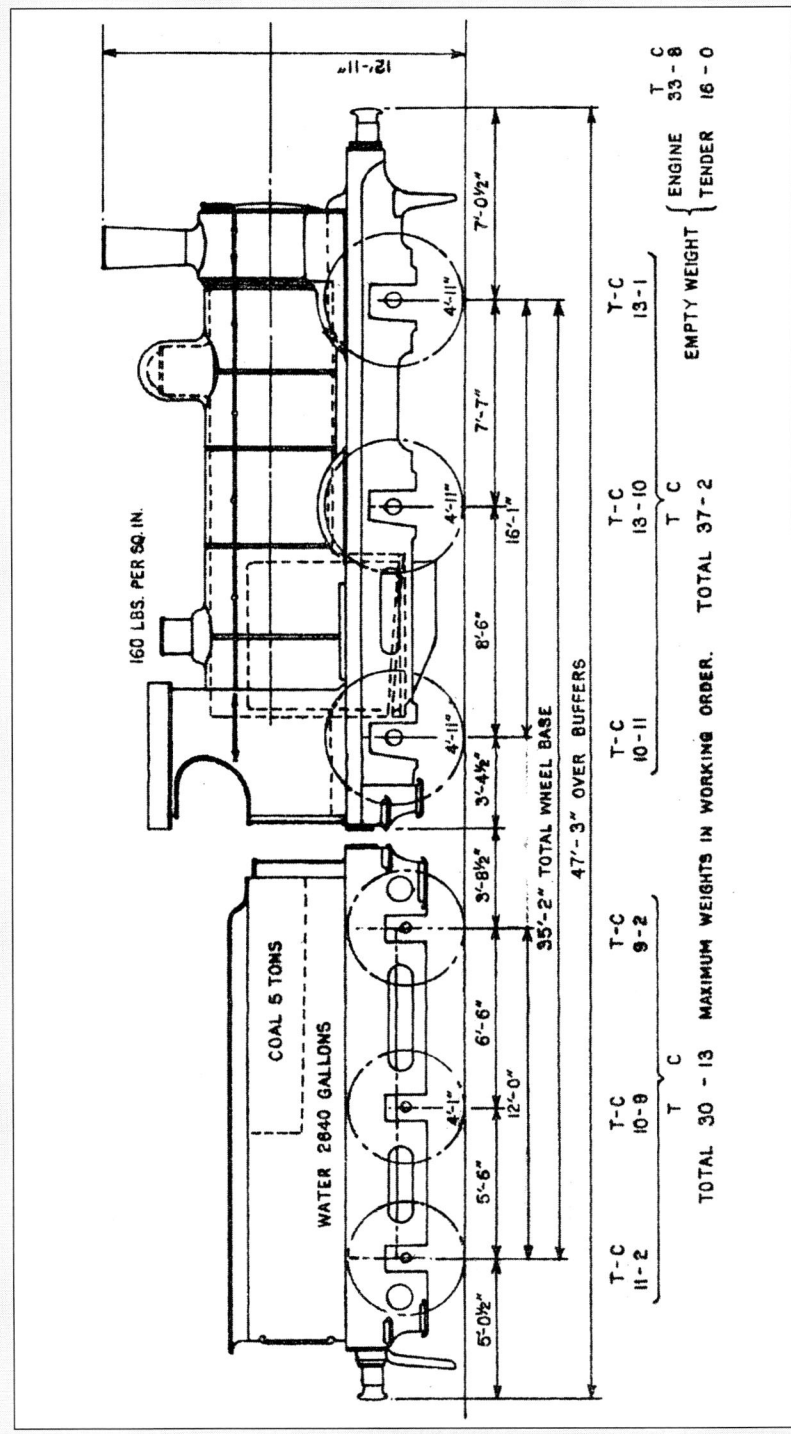

GER 'Y14' class 0-6-0 tender locomotives, later designated 'J15' by the LNER, were long associated with the Snape branch goods services.

LOCOMOTIVES AND ROLLING STOCK

GER No.	LNER 1924 No.	LNER 1946 No.	BR No.	*Condemned*
914	7914	5407	65407	April 1951
915	7915	5408	65408	December 1951
923	7923	–	–	October 1934
933	7933	–	–	March 1936
934	7934	5421	–	March 1948
936	7936	–	–	April 1937
937	7937	5422	65422	July 1955
939	7939	–	–	February 1936
940	7940	5423	–	November 1950
941	7941	5424	65424	December 1959
942	7942	5425	65425	October 1956
943	7943	5426	65426	May 1951

Nos. 65389 and 65478 were amongst the last steam locomotives in use at Ipswich, being retained to work the Snape branch as the timber bridges on the line were incapable of taking the weight of any main line diesel locomotives. Diesel shunting locomotives were unacceptable to the operating authorities as they would have occupied the main line travelling to and from Ipswich for too long a period and thus the 'J15' class reigned supreme to the last.

The leading dimensions of the 'J15' class were:

Cylinders	2 inside	17½ in. x 24 in.
Motion		Stephenson with slide valves
Boiler	Max. dia. outside	4 ft 4 in.
	Barrel length	10 ft 0 in.
Firebox length outside		6 ft 0 in.
Heating surface	Firebox	105.5 sq. ft
	Tubes 242 x 1⅝ in.	1,063.8 sq. ft
	Total	1169.3 sq. ft
Grate area		17.9 sq. ft
Boiler pressure		160 psi
Coupled wheels		4 ft 11 in.
Tender wheels		4 ft 1 in.
Tractive effort		16,942 lb.
Length over buffers		47 ft 3 in.*
Wheelbase	Engine	16 ft 1 in.
	Tender	12 ft 0 in.
	Total	35 ft 2 in.
Weight in working	Engine	37 tons 2 cwt
	Tender	30 tons 13 cwt
	Total	67 tons 15 cwt
Max. axle loading		13 tons 10 cwt
Water capacity		2,640 gallons
Coal capacity		5 tons

* Engine and tender

On occasions after World War II, when a 'J15' class locomotive was not available to work the Snape goods trip, a 'J17' class 0-6-0 tender locomotive took the branch traffic to Snape Junction and left the wagons in the reception siding.

The fragile nature of the underbridges on the Snape branch is evident in this view of 'J15' class No. 65389 as she pulls away from Snape and over the River Alde bridge No. 1109 with her train.
Dr J. Westall/A. Vaughan Collection

With steam shut off and blower on, 'J15' class 0-6-0 No. 65478 negotiates the 1 in 66/249 climb to Snape Junction with the weekdays-only branch goods train. *The late Dr I.C. Allen*

LOCOMOTIVES AND ROLLING STOCK

The traffic was then worked by the Framlingham branch engine, which ran light from Wickham Market with a brake van. The wagons were then tripped to Snape and others returned to the Junction siding or to Wickham Market for collection. For many years the locomotive was invariably an 'F3' class 2-4-2 tank engine of RA3 availability and officially barred from the Snape branch. A total of 50 engines were built between 1893 and 1902 at Stratford works to the design of J. Holden. The GER classified them class 'C32' and they worked initially on the Liverpool Street to Bishop's Stortford semi-fast services and later ran from Liverpool Street to Southend and Southminster. Soon after the turn of the century many were displaced and sent to GER country depots. From then the 'C32' 2-4-2Ts were the mainstay of the Wickham Market to Framlingham branch with an engine outbased from Ipswich. The engines based at Ipswich also worked the Felixstowe, Aldeburgh, Hadleigh and Brightlingsea branches. Locomotives known to have ventured to Snape included:

GER No.	LNER 1924 No.	LNER 1946 No.	BR No.	*Withdrawn*
1042	8042	7143	–	July 1948
1064	8064	7137	–	November 1947
1068	8068	7140	–	March 1949
1079	8079	7127	67127	April 1953

The principal dimensions of the 'F3' class tank locomotives were:

Cylinders		17½ in. x 24 in.
Motion		Stephenson with slide valves
Boiler	Max. diameter	4 ft 4 in.
	Barrel length	10 ft 0 in.
Firebox		5 ft 5 in.
Heating surface	Tubes 242 x 1⅝ in.	1,063.8 sq. ft
	Firebox	100.9 sq. ft
	Total	1164.7 sq. ft
Grate area		18.0 sq. ft
Boiler pressure		160 psi
Leading wheels		4 ft 0 in.
Driving wheels		5 ft 8 in.
Trailing wheels		4 ft 0 in.
Tractive effort		14,700 lb.
Length over buffers		34 ft 10 in.
Wheelbase		23 ft 3 in.
Weight in working order		58 tons 12 cwt
Max. axle loading		15 tons 6 cwt
Water capacity		1,460 gallons
Coal capacity		3 tons 5 cwt

During World War II, 15 'F4' class and one 'F5' class 2-4-2 tank locomotives were loaned to the Government for hauling coastal defence armoured trains. The initial 40 members of the 'M15' class had entered service between 1884 and 1887 to the design of T.W. Worsdell. Between 1903 and 1909 a further 120 locomotives were built, and from 1911 until 1920 the GER rebuilt 30 engines

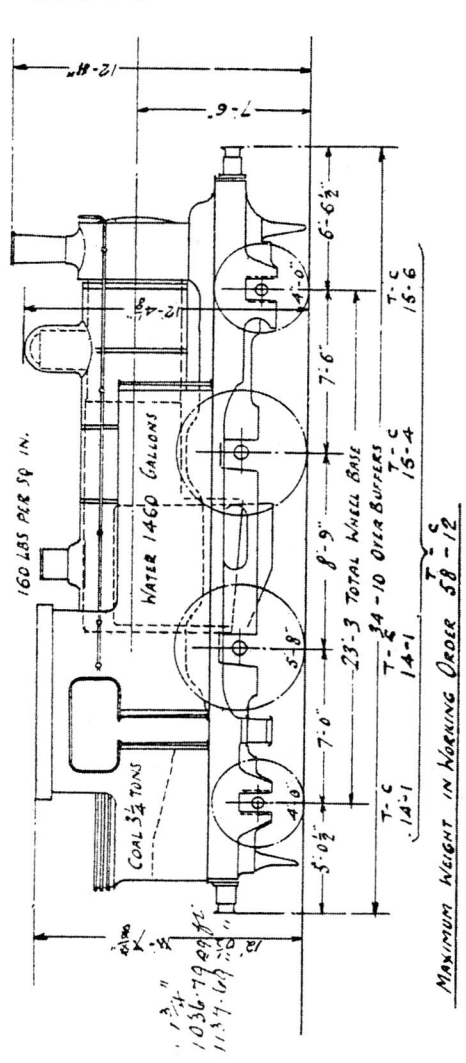

GER 'C32' class 2-4-2 tank locomotives, later designated 'F3' by the LNER, occasionally worked the Snape branch goods services.

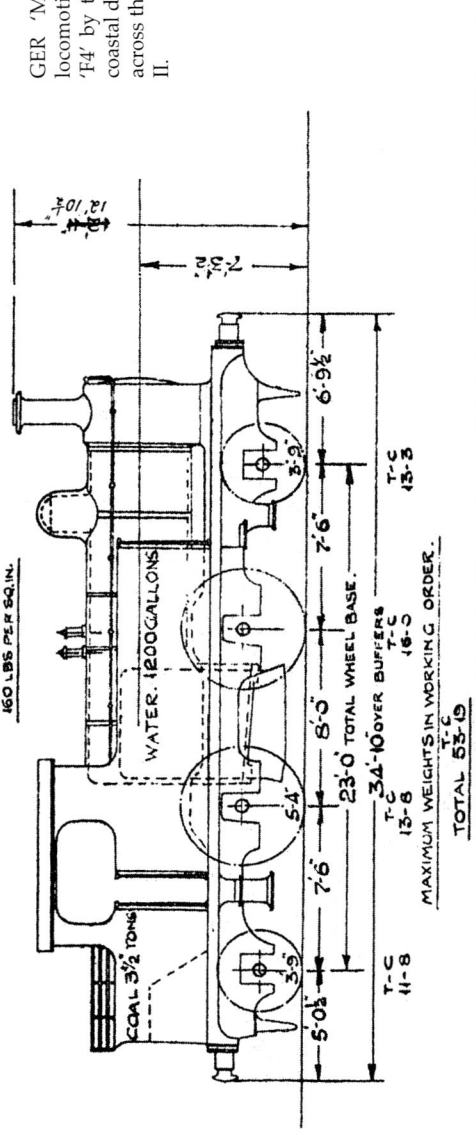

GER 'M15' class 2-4-2 tank locomotives, later designated 'F4' by the LNER, worked the coastal defence armoured trains across the branch in World War II.

with higher boiler pressure and designated them 'M15R'. The earliest built locomotives were all condemned by 1929, whilst the LNER classified the 'M15s' class 'F4 'and rebuilt engines class 'F5'. They were nicknamed 'Gobblers' because the original engines had a voracious appetite for coal and although improvements were made the name persisted. Between June 1940 and July 1943 the Snape branch, together with the neighbouring Framlingham and Aldeburgh lines, were regularly patrolled by the coastal defence trains, initially by train D powered by 'F4' class No. 7178 based at Ipswich, and then by train C hauled by 'F4' class No. 7214. Because of the weight of the train a speed limit of 5 mph was enforced over the three bridges on the Snape branch and after the first few trips the local District Engineer was highly dubious of the train traversing the line at all. He was initially persuaded that the runs were for the national protection of the country but as the months progressed the trips across the branch were reduced considerably and then ceased altogether. The following 'F4' class locomotives travelled across the Snape branch:

GER No.	LNER 1924 No.	LNER 1946 No.	BR No.	Condemned
178	7178	7173	–	April 1948
214	7214	7162	67162	August 1955

The leading dimensions of the 'F4' class were:

Cylinders	2 inside	17½ in. x 24 in.
Motion		Stephenson with slide valves
Boiler	Max. dia. outside	4 ft 2 in.
	Barrel length	10 ft 2½ in.
Firebox length outside		5 ft 5 in.
Heating surface	Firebox	98.4 sq. ft
	Tubes 227 x 1⅝ in.	1018.0 sq. ft
	Total	1116.4 sq. ft
Grate area		15.3 sq. ft
Boiler pressure		160 psi
Leading wheels		3 ft 9 in.
Coupled wheels		5 ft 4 in.
Trailing wheels		3 ft 9 in.
Tractive effort		15,618 lb.
Length over buffers		34 ft 10 in.
Wheelbase		23 ft 0 in.
Weight in working order		51 tons 11 cwt
Max. axle loading		14 tons 18 cwt
Water capacity		1,200 gallons
Coal capacity		3 tons 10 cwt

The only other visitors to the Snape branch were 'E4' class 2-4-0 tender locomotives. No. 2782, later 62782, was recorded working the goods service in 1947 but was rather overloaded by the time the train reached Wickham Market, whilst No. 62797 worked the only passenger train to traverse the line, the Railway Enthusiasts' Club 'Suffolk Venturer' rail tour on 30th September, 1956. The 100 'T26' class locomotives were built at Stratford works to the design of

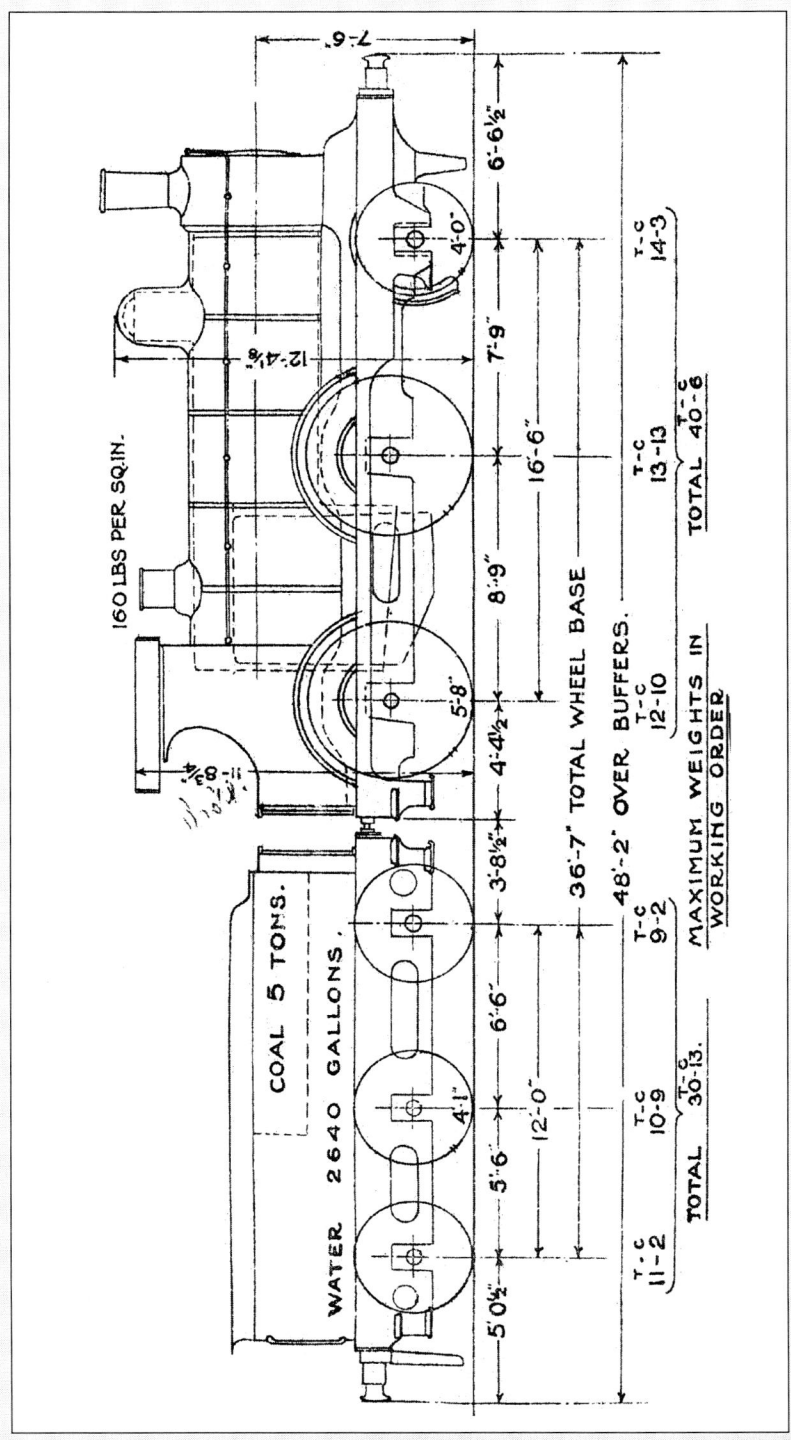

GER 'T26' class 2-4-0 tender locomotives, later designated 'E4' by the LNER.

James Holden between 1891 and 1902 and nicknamed 'Intermediates'. The engines were used on cross-country routes and mixed traffic workings and were reclassified 'E4' by the LNER after grouping. Ipswich district engines had over the years often worked on the East Suffolk branches and might indeed have deputised on other Snape branch workings. Details of the engines that worked to Snape were:

GER No.	LNER 1924 No.	LNER 1946 No.	BR No.	*Withdrawn*
416	7416	2797	62797	March 1958
466	7466	2782	62782	November 1954

The principal dimensions of the 'E4' class were:

Cylinders		17½ in. x 24 in.
Motion		Stephenson with slide valves
Boiler	Max. diameter	4 ft 4 in.
	Barrel length	10 ft 0 in.
Firebox		6 ft 0 in.
Heating surface	Tubes 242 x 1⅝ in.	1,063.8 sq. ft
	Firebox	100.9 sq. ft
	Total	1164.7 sq. ft
Grate area		18.0 sq. ft
Boiler pressure		160 psi
Leading wheels		4 ft 0 in.
Driving wheels		5 ft 8 in.
Tractive effort		14,700 lb.
Length over buffers		48 ft 2 in.*
Wheelbase		16 ft 6 in.
Weight in working order		40 tons 6 cwt
Max. axle loading		14 tons 3 cwt
Tender	Wheelbase	12 ft 0 in.
	Wheel diameter	4 ft 1 in.
	Weight in working order	30 tons 13 cwt
	Water capacity	2,640 gallons
	Coal capacity	5 tons

* Engine and tender

With the exception of the early years, when Norwich and Yarmouth engines and men worked some of the goods services, motive power for the Snape branch was always provided by Ipswich shed, later coded 32B by British Railways. No engine was outbased at Snape and the line was worked on an out and back basis each day. Ipswich footplate crews initially 'signed the road' for the branch but within a year because of the reduction of main line freight services, it was decided the Framlingham-based engine and men would also work the line. Although this was later superseded, the Framlingham men continued to retain their route knowledge. Train crews, noted for their love of tea, often topped up their tea can with boiling water from the signalman's kettle at Snape Junction signal box before working the train down the branch. Because of the flat terrain, on a fine day the signalman could watch the progress of the

'E4' class 2-4-0 tender locomotive No. 2782 at Dereham shed in 1946. The following year when allocated to Ipswich it worked on the Snape goods service without much success as by the time the train reached Wickham Market the engine was overloaded. *Author's Collection*

'E4' class 2-4-0 tender locomotives saw only occasional use on the Snape branch. In the event of the non- availability of a 'J15' class locomotive, 'E4' No 2782, later 62782, when based at Ipswich in 1947, was pressed into service on the Saxmundham and Snape goods turn. With her larger driving wheels the engine had difficulty working the train and the experiment was soon concluded. A member of the class returned to the Snape line on 30th September, 1956, when No. 62797 hauled the Railway Enthusiasts' Club 'Suffolk Venturer' special train across the branch. Unfortunately despite being in immaculate external condition, she was steaming badly and ran out of steam on the return working from Snape. Here No. 62797 awaits assistance with her train at Snape Junction. *The Late H.C. Casserley*

up goods working from Snape and by the time the train was passing the branch fixed distant, the kettle was at boiling point so that a brew could be made before the train continued to Ipswich.

Initially the engine working the booked branch service carried no headlamp by day and one white light at the base of the chimney by night. Special trains only carried lights at night with the engine displaying a white light at the base of the chimney and another on the buffer beam, if fitted with a lamp bracket or presumably attached to the coupling. By 1875 the headcode for ordinary trains was the same, but special trains carried a white disc at the base of the chimney by day and two white lights at night. By the 1890s the engine working the Snape branch carried a headcode for an ordinary goods train of a green disc with white outer rim on the lamp iron over the right-hand buffer and a white disc on the lamp iron over the left-hand buffer. By 1906 this had altered to three white discs, one under the chimney, one in the centre of the buffer beam and one over the left hand buffer. In 1919 the headcode was rationalised to one white disc over the left-hand buffer. After Grouping the designated Railway Clearing House class headcode was carried. During the hours of darkness and fog or falling snow appropriate oil headlamps were carried in place of the discs. The headcode was supposedly to be carried at all times but in practice the engine often carried no headcode at all, especially on the branch.

The whistle code to be sounded for trains approaching Snape Junction in GER days was 1 distinct sound for the main line and 3 distinct sounds for trains using the Snape branch. The LNER made no provision for a special whistle code at Snape Junction.

In the event of a derailment or breakdown on the goods line, the Ipswich breakdown vans were delegated to attend, and later 20 ton steam crane No. 961903 with its attendant train was used for any mishap. Built by the GER in 1908 as No. 5A the crane received No. 961903 in the LNER 1938 renumbering scheme, and was later renumbered 132 by British Railways before being condemned in 1967. Although having an RA4 route availability the crane was permitted to run across RA2 routes at reduced speed. Other GE section breakdown vehicles, 45 ton steam crane No. 961606 allocated to Cambridge and 35 ton steam crane No. 961601 allocated to Stratford, were prohibited from working across the branch.

Wagons

As the Snape branch was a freight-only line, a short description of rolling stock provided by the ECR, GER and LNER for the conveyance of goods is appropriate. The details are not exhaustive but give guidance as to the general user vehicles used on the branch trains. The restricted accommodation at Snape, including the 13 ft 6 in.-diameter wagon turntable at the entrance to the maltings, ensured that the size and variety of goods stock used on the branch was limited.

The wagons used by the ECR were wooden open vehicles with side doors and fitted with dumb buffers. Where grain, straw or merchandise was

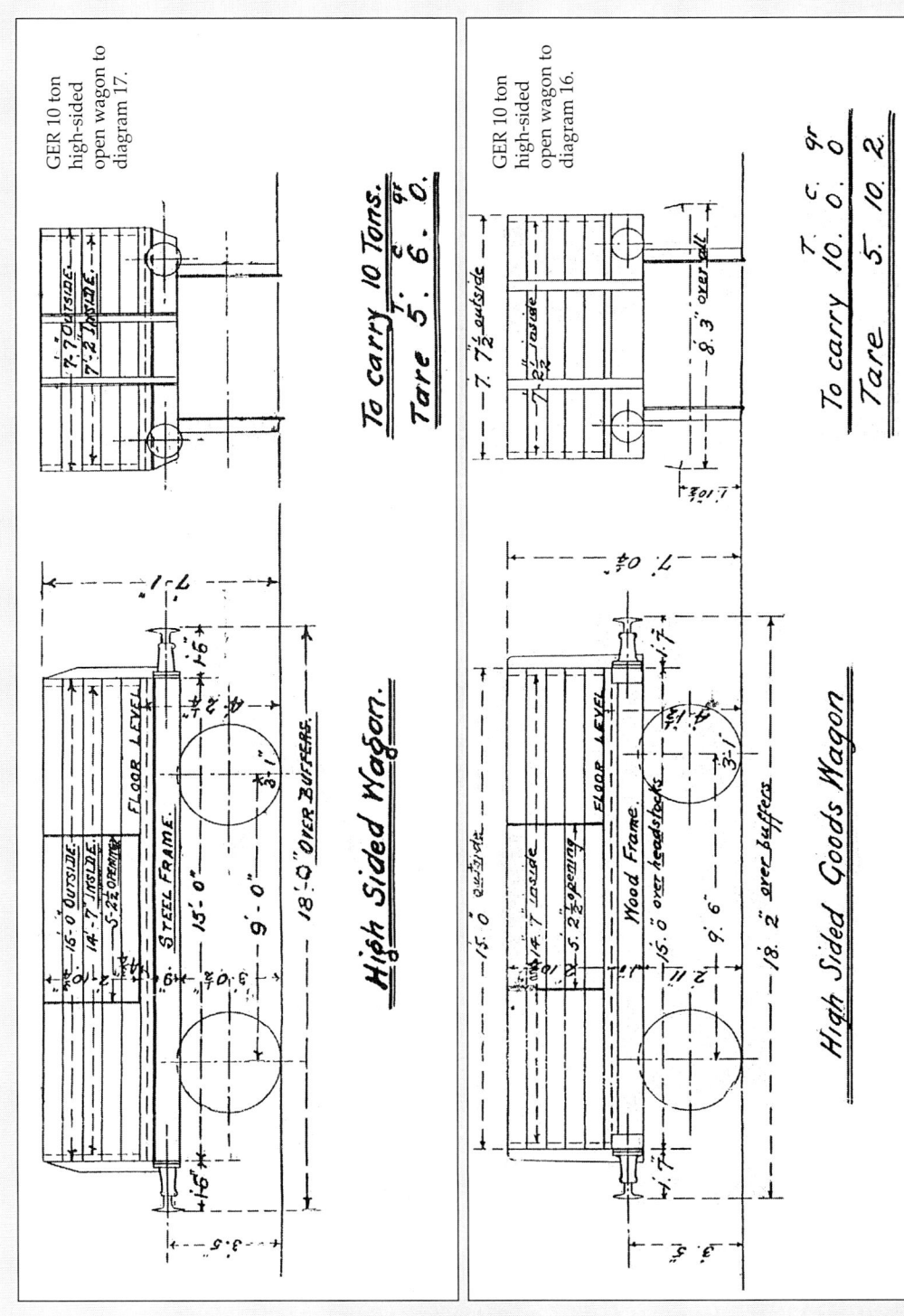

LOCOMOTIVES AND ROLLING STOCK

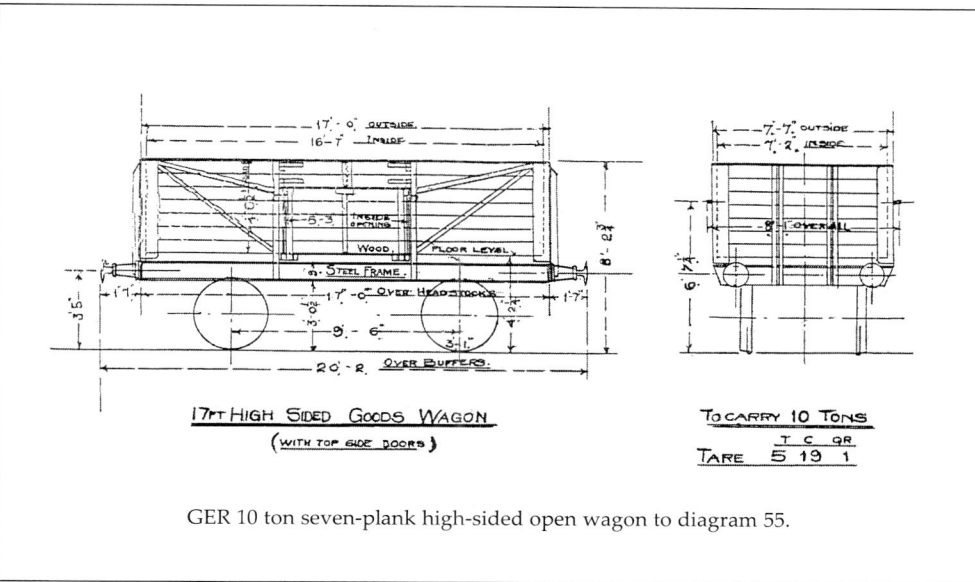

GER 10 ton seven-plank high-sided open wagon to diagram 55.

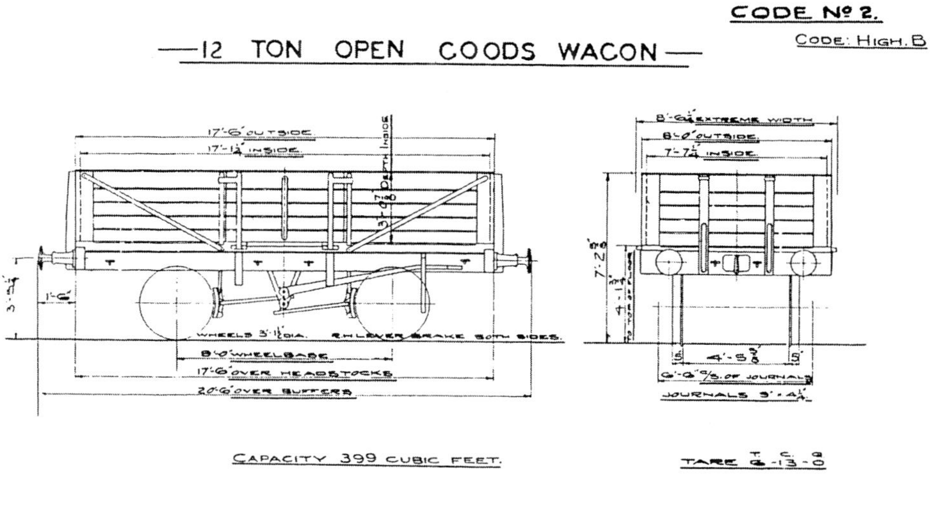

LNER 12 ton open goods wagon to code 2.

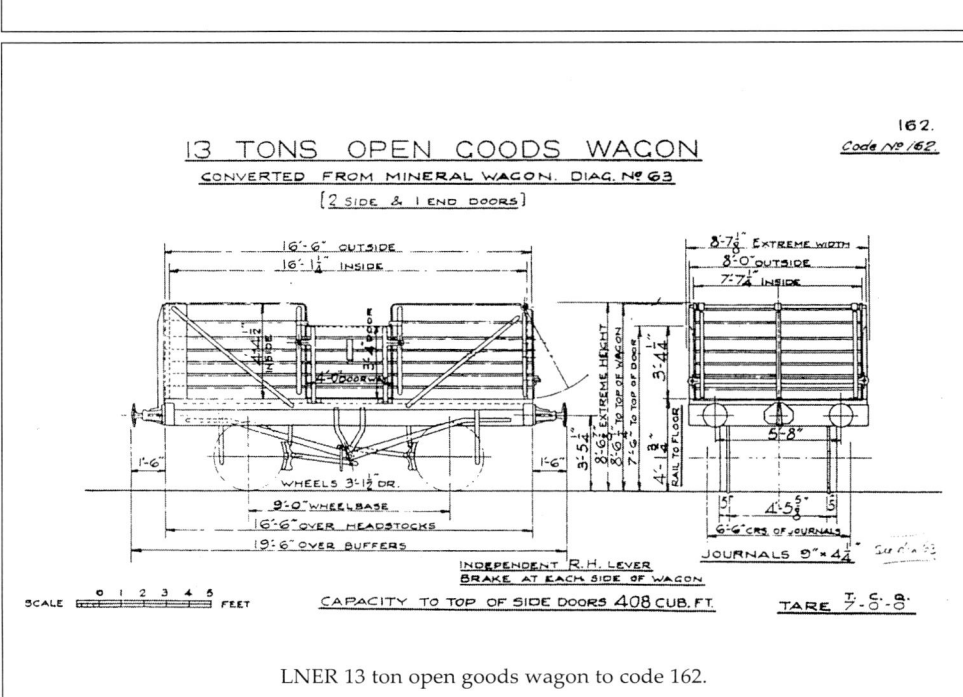

LNER 12 ton open goods wagon to code 91.

LNER 13 ton open goods wagon to code 162.

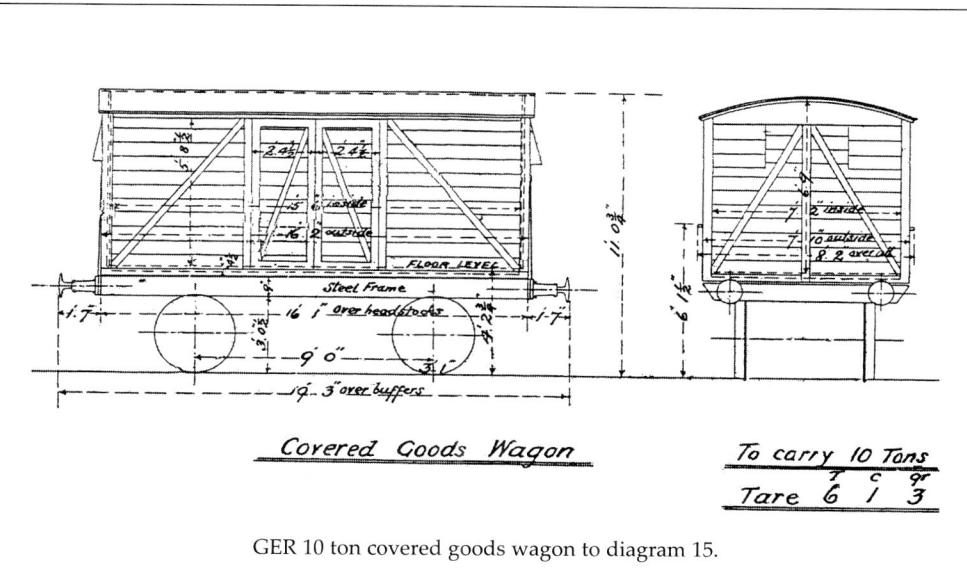

GER 10 ton covered goods wagon to diagram 15.

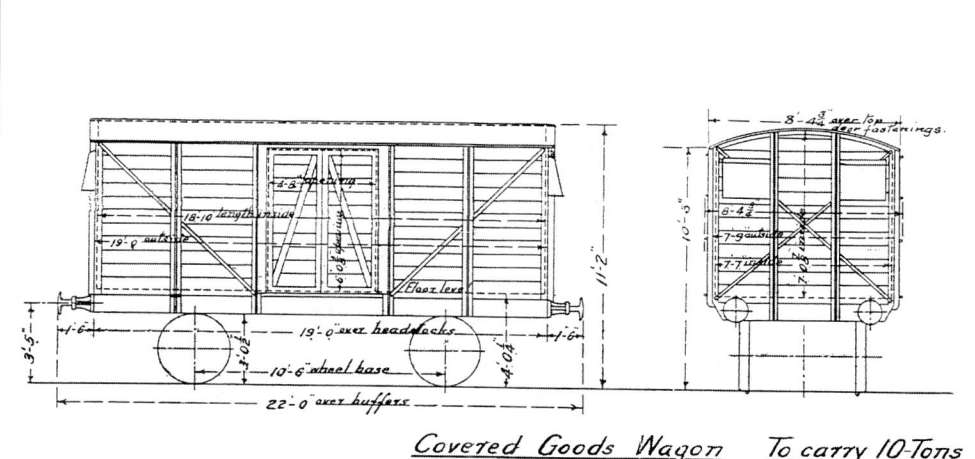

GER 10 ton covered goods wagon to diagram 72.

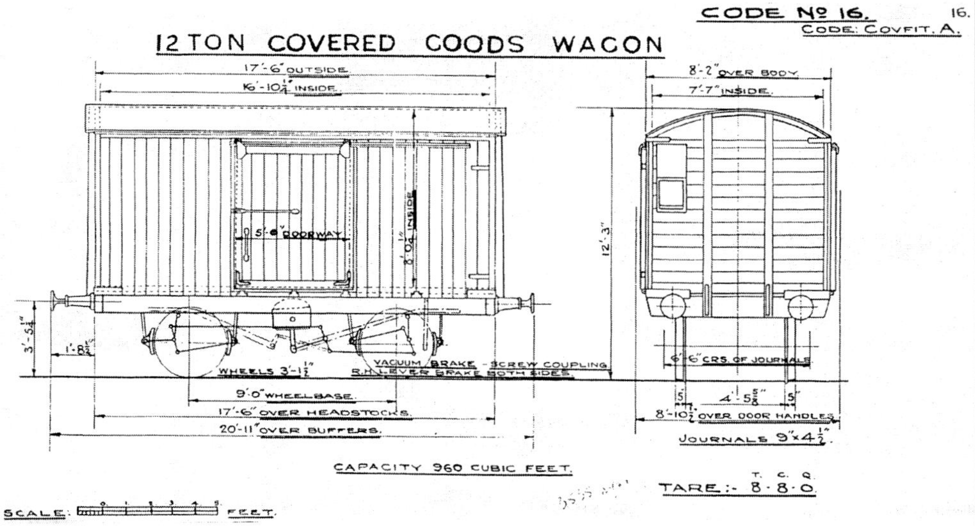

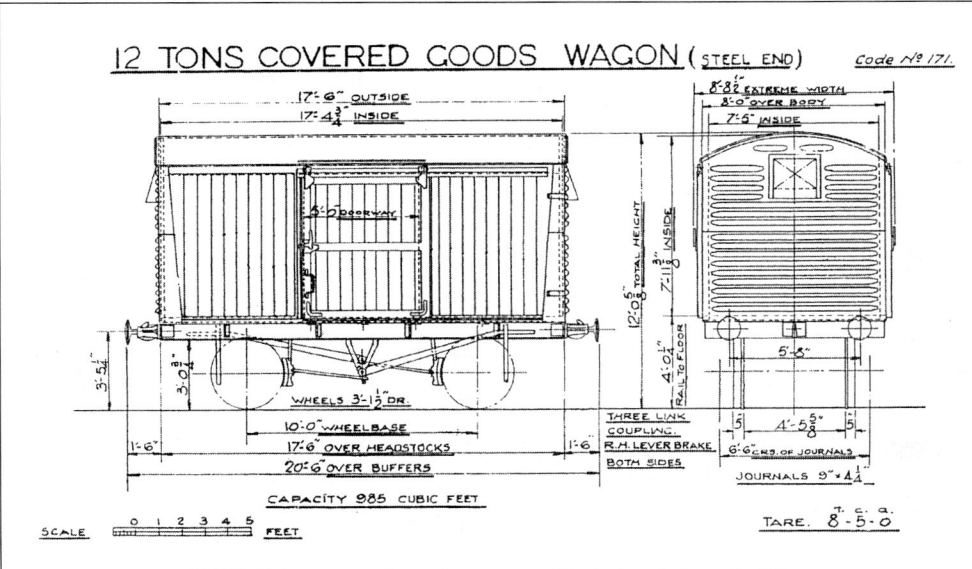

LNER 12 ton covered goods wagon to code 16.

LNER 12 ton covered goods wagon with steel ends to code 171.

susceptible to wet weather, a tarpaulin sheet was utilised to protect the contents of the wagon. The brake van at the tail of the train would have been a 10 ton vehicle. In the years prior to the turn of the century the GE company utilised four-plank-bodied, open wagons with wooden frames, dating from 1882, for conveyance of general merchandise and minerals. From 1887, these wagons were gradually superseded by five-plank, 9 ton capacity (later 10 ton) opens, to diagram 16 with 9 ft 6 in. wheelbase and measuring 15 ft 0 in. over headstocks. Later 10 ton, five-plank open wagons to diagram 17, with a length of 15 ft 0 in. over headstocks and 9 ft 0 in. wheelbase, were also used. Another variation was the use of 10 ton, seven-plank opens to diagram 55, measuring 17 ft 0 in. over headstocks and 9 ft 6 in. wheelbase for vegetable and root traffic. For fruit and perishable traffic, 10 ton ventilated vans to diagram 15 were provided, measuring 16 ft 1 in. over headstocks, with a 9 ft 0 in. wheelbase and overall height of 11 ft 0¾ in. Later covered goods vans to diagram 47 were also utilised. They measured 17 ft 3 in. over headstocks, had a wheelbase of 10 ft 6 in. and were 11 ft 2 in. in height. A third variation was the 10 ton capacity covered goods wagon to diagram 72, which measured 19 ft 0 in. over headstocks whilst maintaining a 10 ft 6 in. wheelbase. The small amount of cattle traffic to and from Snape would have brought three types of cattle wagon to the branch. The first of 8 ton capacity to diagram 5 was 18 ft 7 in. over headstocks, had a 10 ft 6 in. wheelbase and was 10 ft 10¾ in. in height. The second to diagram 6 was of 9 ton capacity and measured 19 ft 0 in. over headstocks with a 10 ft 6 in. wheelbase and overall height of 10 ft 10½ in. The third GE variation of cattle wagon to diagram 7 was of 10 tons capacity, 19 ft 3 in. over headstocks with 10 ft 6 in. wheelbase and overall height of 11 ft 2 in. At the tail of the train was usually a 20 ton four-wheel brake van to GE diagram 56, measuring 17 ft 6 in. over headstocks, a 10 ft 3 in. wheelbase and 3 ft 1 in. diameter wheels. In addition many wagons owned by other companies were used to deliver and collect agricultural and maltings traffic, whilst coal and coke supplies came in private owner coal wagons. These fell into two categories, those belonging to the collieries consigning the coal, and merchants and coal factors wagons, which were loaded at the collieries.

After Grouping the GER wagons continued to be utilised but gradually LNER standard designed wagons made an appearance. The most numerous were probably the 12 ton, five-plank opens with an 8 ft 0 in. wheelbase to code 2, and 12 ton, six-plank open with 10 ft 0 in. wheelbase to code 91 built after 1932. Later types included the 13 ton, seven-plank open wagon to code 162 measuring 16 ft 6 in. over headstocks and with a 9 ft 0 in. wheelbase. All were used on vegetable and sugar beet traffic. Fitted and unfitted 12 ton, 9 ft 0 in. wheelbase covered vans to code 16 conveyed perishable goods, fruit and malt and later some were designated for fruit traffic only. From 1934 12 ton capacity vans to code 171, with steel underframe and pressed corrugated steel ends, were introduced whilst at the same time the wheelbase was extended to a length of 10 feet. Specific fruit vans with both 9 ft and 10 ft wheelbase also saw service on the Snape branch for malt traffic. Agricultural machinery destined for the maltings or local farms was delivered to Snape on 12 ton Lowfit wagons, with 10 ft wheelbase and overall length over headstocks of 17 ft 6 in. Larger machinery would have arrived or departed on one of the ex-GER 14

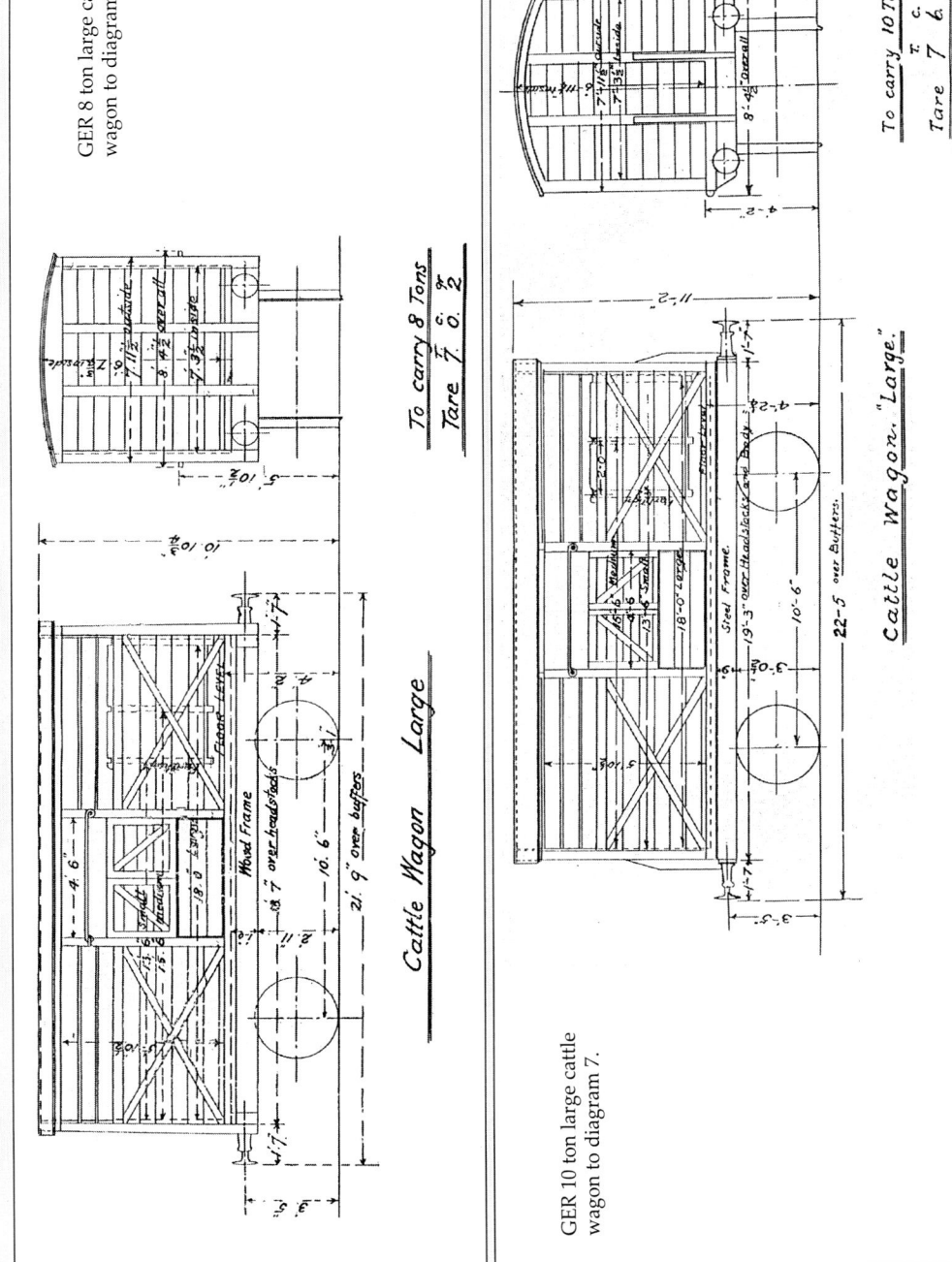

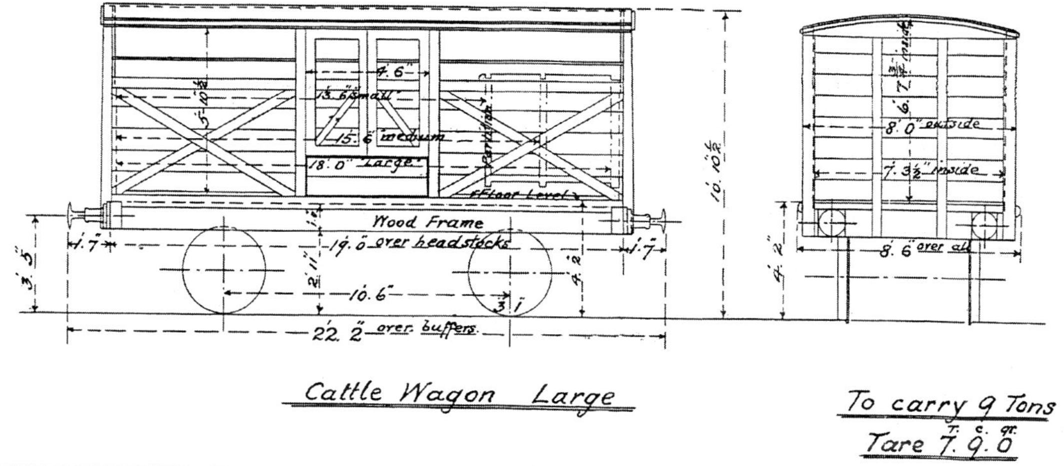

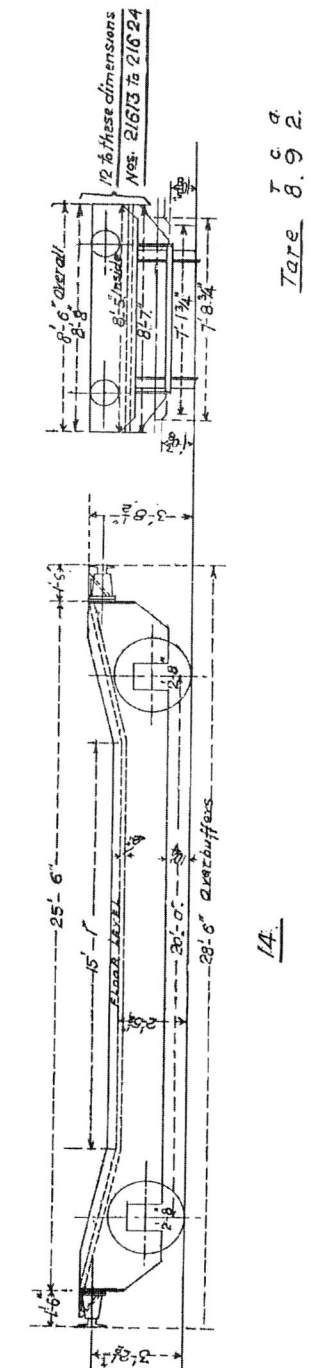

GER 9 ton large cattle wagon to diagram 6.

GER 14 ton machine wagon to diagram 75.

GER 20 ton goods brake van to diagram 56.

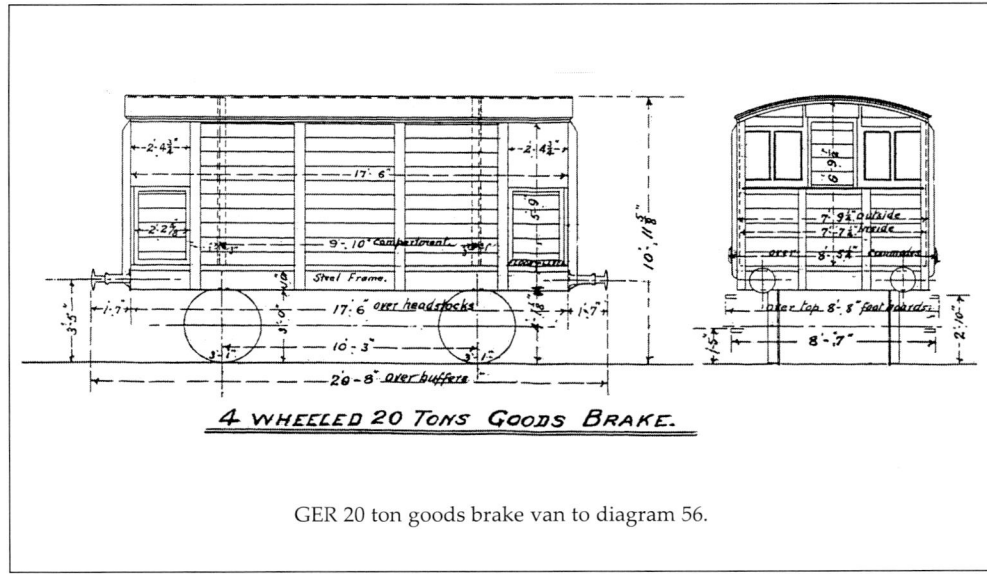

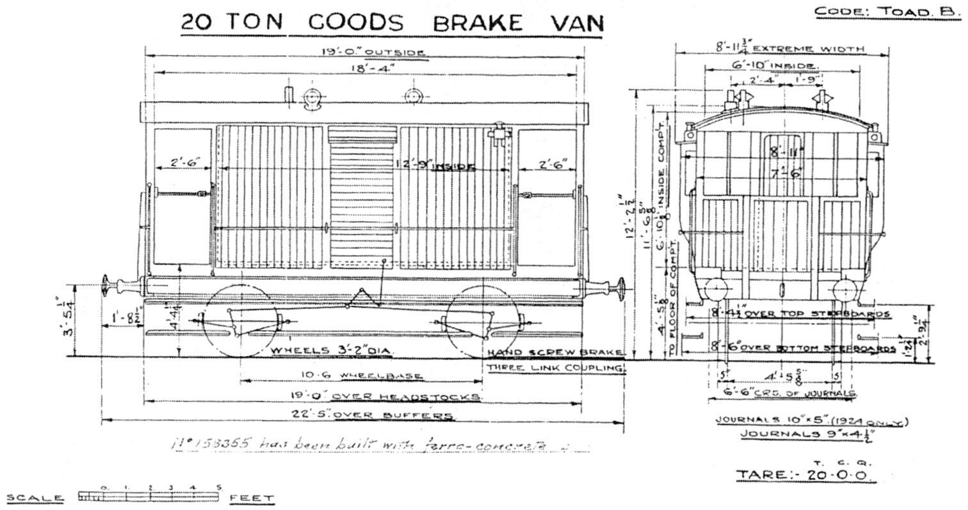

LNER 20 ton goods brake van 'Toad B' to code 34.

ton, 25 ft 6 in. 'Mac K2' machinery wagons to diagram 75 and later LNER builds. LNER brake vans provided for the branch included 20 ton 'Toad B' to code 34 and 'Toad E' to code 64 vehicles with 10 ft 6 in. wheelbase and measuring 22 ft 5 in. over buffers. Later 'Toad D' brake vans to code 61 with 16 ft wheelbase and measuring 27 ft 5 in. over buffers were employed. Although wagons with a wheelbase exceeding 13 ft 6 in. were permitted on the Snape branch they were not allowed to pass over the turntable at the end of the line and neither were they permitted to be loaded at the terminus. After nationalisation many of the older wooden vehicles were scrapped and much of the traffic conveyed in open wagons was carried in the standard 16 ton all steel mineral vehicles.

An interesting survivor at Snape, albeit in derelict condition, was a former GER 16 ft 2 in.-long standard covered goods wagon No. 6102, built in the mid-1890s at Stratford. After passing to the LNER, when it was renumbered 606102, it was withdrawn in the early 1930s and acquired by Swonnell's to serve as a mobile loading platform in the maltings. After the closure of the branch it graced the front of the maltings but immediately prior to Her Majesty the Queen opening the new concert hall in 1967 it was, not surprisingly, moved to the other side of the road and dumped on the site of the former goods station, where it remains to this day.

In GER days the body, solebars and headstocks of the open wagons were painted slate grey whilst the ironwork below solebar level, buffer guides, buffers, drawbars, drawbar plates and couplings were black. Lettering was white. Brake vans had vermilion headstocks. The LNER wagon livery was grey for non-fitted wagons and covered vans whilst all vehicles fitted with automatic brakes, including brake vans, were painted brown red oxide which changed to bauxite around 1940. Similar liveries were carried in BR days.

The maintenance of the wagon stock used on the branch was carried out at the wagon repair shops at Ipswich. In the event of the failure or defect of a wagon on the branch, a travelling wagon repairer carried out repairs at Snape or Snape Junction.

S. Swonnell & Sons Ltd owned a small fleet of 10 ton six-plank open wagons with side and end doors, the top plank above the side door being cut away. The vehicles were mounted on spoked wheels with grease axleboxes and had brakes and brake levers on one side only. It is uncertain how many vehicles Swonnell's owned, but the body and solebar were painted red oxide with white lettering, shaded black. The wheels and running gear were black. A survivor found at Swonnell's maltings at Oulton Broad, located a quarter of a mile west of Oulton Broad, later Oulton Broad North station on the GER Reedham to Lowestoft line, carried the number 20 and SNAPE on the side planks. The vehicle was built in 1898 and registered with the Midland Railway but was actually owned by Moy's Wagons of Peterborough. This suggests that Swonnell's hired this wagon, and indeed others. The state of dereliction when found at Oulton Broad suggests it had not been used since the mid-1930s. It is uncertain how long the vehicle had been at Oulton Broad but transfer must have been made via the Snape branch and the East Suffolk main line. The wagon was probably initially used to convey the specialist coal for malting. The company also owned some wagons for internal use and these were hauled by horses and in later years a tractor, both being used to transfer wagons about the yard and, via the turntable, across the road to the main line.

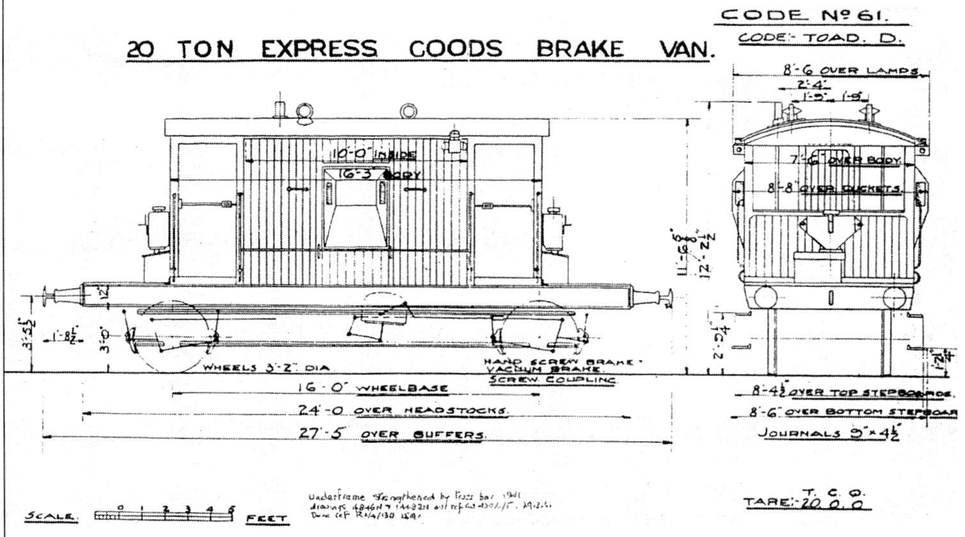

LNER 20 ton goods brake van 'Toad D' to code 61.

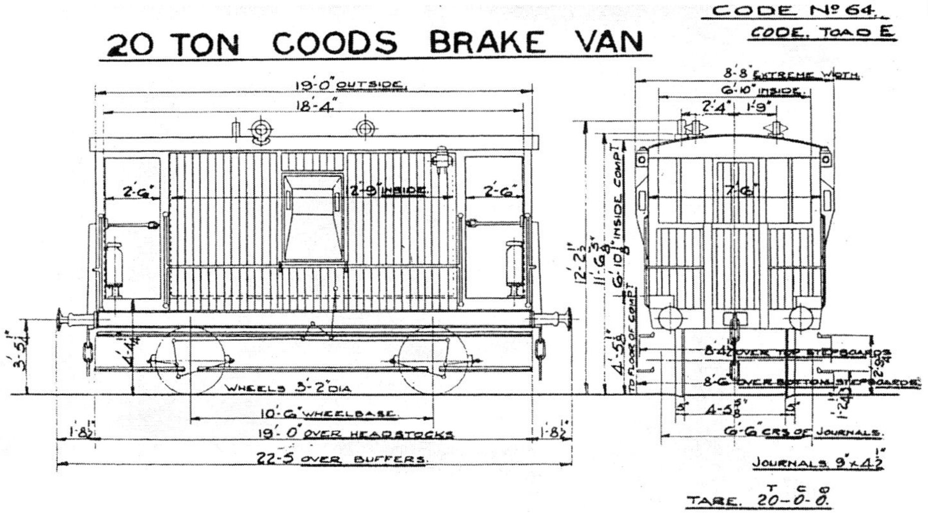

LNER 20 ton goods brake van 'Toad E' to code 64.

LOCOMOTIVES AND ROLLING STOCK

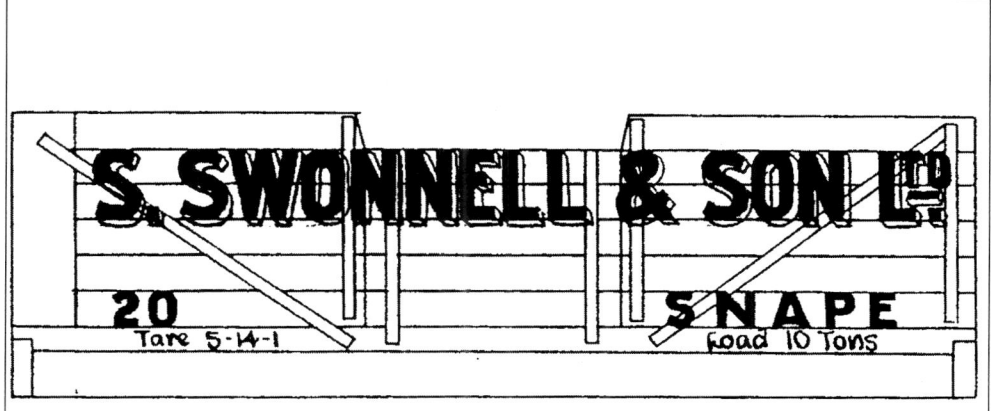

Drawing of Swonnell & Sons wagon No 20.

Former GER covered van No. 6102, withdrawn in the 1930s, at Snape maltings on 17th March, 1963 where it was used as a mobile loading platform. Just before Her Majesty Queen Elizabeth II visited Snape to open the new concert hall in June 1967, the vehicle was moved from the maltings to the old station site where it was out of sight and mind. *J. Watling*

The shunter stands guard on the approach to Snape maltings as the Fordson tractor shunts two open wagons towards the goods yard in 1959. By this time the maltings were becoming outdated and registered to most as a charming piece of Victorian enterprise. S. Swonnell & Sons had long ceased receiving barley and dispatching malt by rail and only coal and coke supplies were received in open wagons. Note the disused connection from the reception siding in the foreground.

Appendix One

Level Crossings

No.	Location	Mileage from Liverpool Street M. Ch.		Local Name	Status
1	Snape Junction & Snape	88	24	Botany Wood	footpath
2	Snape Junction & Snape	88	48		occupation
3	Snape Junction & Snape	88	57	Groom's	occupation
4	Snape Junction & Snape	88	76		occupation
5	Snape Junction & Snape	89	21		occupation
6	Snape Junction & Snape	89	29	River Alde	footpath
7	Snape Station	89	40	Tunstall Road	public road

Snape goods station in 1958 viewed from the archway of the maltings. The remains of the goods shed are on the left. The structure was found to be in a poor state of repair in 1957 and was demolished leaving only the goods office standing. The wagon turntable fronting the archway and associated sidings along the frontage of the maltings were also removed by this date. The turntable was replaced by a section of plain track leaving just one access line for wagons to be shunted into and out of the maltings.   *The late B.D.J. Walsh*

Appendix Two

Bridges

Bridge No.	Location	Mileage m. ch.	Local Name	Under or Over	Type	Spans	Square Span between abutments or supports ft. in.	Skew Span between abutments or supports ft. in.	Depth of construction ft. in.	Distance from road or surface of water to rail ft. in.	Construction
1107	Snape Junction & Snape	88 61	Groom's	Under	Stream	1	11 7	13 6	3 3	4 5	Timber piles Timber superstructure
1108	Snape Junction & Snape	89 00	-	Under	Stream	3	15 5 16 0 15 8	- -	3 1	6 2	Timber piles Timber superstructure
1109	Snape Junction & Snape	89 28	Snape River	Under	River Alde	7	20 3 20 7 20 7 21 0 21 0 21 0 21 2	- -	3 9	5 10 at High Water	Timber piles Timber superstructure

Acknowledgements

The publication of this history would not have been possible without the help of many people who have been kind enough to assist. In particular I should like to thank

The late A.R. Cox
The late W. Fenton
The late G. Woodcock
The late Dr I.C. Allen
John Watling
Dave Hoser
The late Bernard Walsh
Dave Taylor
Alan Keeler
Doug Stephenson
John Petrie
The late Canon C. Bayes
The late G. Pember
The late P. Proud

also staff of the former Ipswich Motive Power Depot and the many active and retired railway staff of the Ipswich District, some of whom worked on the Snape branch.

Thanks are also due to the Public Record Office (now National Archives), British Railways, Eastern Region, The House of Lords Record Office, The British Library Newspaper Library, Suffolk County Record Office, Ipswich and members of the Great Eastern Railway Society.

'J15' class No. 65478 propels wagons into Snape using the main single line over the river bridge as a headshunt. Because of the lack of run round facilities, locomotives working the branch normally propelled the train from Snape Junction.   *The late Dr I.C. Allen*

Bibliography

General Works

Aldrich, C.L., *GER Locomotives*
Allen, C.J., *The Great Eastern Railway*, Ian Allan
Gordon, D.I., *Regional History of the Railways of Great Britain Vol. 5*, David & Charles
RCTS, *Locomotives of the LNER*
Simper R., *Over Snape Bridge*, East Anglia Magazines Ltd

Periodicals

Bradshaw's Railway Guide
Bradshaw's Railway Manual
British Railways, Eastern Region Magazine
East Anglia Magazine
Great Eastern Railway Magazine
Locomotive Carriage and Wagon Review
Locomotive Magazine
LNER Magazine
Railway Magazine
Railway World
Railway Year Book
Trains Illustrated

Newspapers

East Anglian Daily Times
Ipswich Journal
Suffolk Chronicle

Also Minute Books of the East Suffolk Railway (Extracts)
         Eastern Counties Railway
         Great Eastern Railway
         London & North Eastern Railway

Working Timetables: ECR, GER, LNER and BR (ER).
Appendices to Working Timetables: GER, LNER and BR (ER).